Behind Sad Eyes

The Life of

George Harrison

Behind
Sad
Eyes

The Life of
George Harrison

Marc Shapiro

ST. MARTIN'S PRESS
NEW YORK

www.stmartins.com

Library of Congress Cataloging-in-Publication Data

Shapiro, Marc.
     Behind sad eyes : the Life of George Harrison / Marc Shapiro.—1st ed.
         p. cm.
     Includes bibliographical references and discography.
     ISBN 0-312-30109-X
     1. Harrison, George, 1943–2001.   2. Rock musicians—England—
   Biography.   I. Title.

ML420.H167 S53 2002
782.42166'092—dc21
[B]

                                                                2001058561

First Edition: May 2002

10   9   8   7   6   5   4   3   2   1

Contents

Acknowledgments

Thanks to:

My wife, Nancy, and daughter, Rachael: for the light. Agent Lori Perkins: for the hustle. Bennie, Freda, and Selma: for the love. Marc Resnick: for the call to duty. Mike Kirby, Steve Ross, the rock gods at Poo Bah, and the paid-up members of the No Bullshit Squad. War all that is just in the world. And thanks to George Harrison: for the life. No Beatle was harmed or interviewed in the writing of this book.

Introduction
Behind Sad Eyes

George Harrison may have been the happiest person on the planet. But you could not tell that by looking into his eyes.

Contemplative? Yes. Enlightened? Occasionally. Resigned? Certainly. But the twinkle of joy? The glint of happiness? In the case of George Harrison, it was never really there. Even during the heyday of the Beatles, when anything and everything seemed possible, there was something around the edges of Harrison's seemingly set-in-stone, wide-eyed, and bemused stare that said, *This is not real*, and that he was not comfortable with living this fantasy life.

The smiles during the endless press conferences always seemed a bit too forced and a bit too false. During his time as part of the Beatles, the look on George's face perhaps reflected the desire to slow down while his life was rushing past him at the speed of light. Did he ever look content? Yes. There were those moments, captured in the millions of photographs taken of him, when he was alone at his home or on the street, signing an autograph for an adoring fan, where the emotions of somebody who was enjoying life crept through. And once again, the telltale evidence was in the eyes.

George Harrison had gone through a lot since the days when his passion for music put him on the road to stardom and, on the eve of 2002, the fates, karma, and his own personal and professional choices combined to put sadness in those puppy-dog eyes. In the classic sense, George Harrison had arrived, well into his fifth decade, a bloodied but ultimately unbowed creation: a long-haired, pop icon–cum–Don Quixote who has tilted at one too many windmills and who has won, but, just as often, also lost.

As the subject of a celebrity biography, it all sounds too much like work, heavy on the melancholy and more than a bit downbeat. In *Behind Sad Eyes: The George Harrison Story*, don't look for the fairy-tale ending or an odyssey without a bump in the road. Because to cloak the life and times of George Harrison in anything but flawed and imperfect terms would be a gross miscarriage of history and of the truth. And, it would probably not make George happy.

Because what made George Harrison the endearing icon and the subject of just as much conjecture and speculation as blind fan praise, well beyond the expected curiosity attached to his Beatles years, are his emotional and human imperfections. Hardly a badge of honor but rather a badge of living, Harrison's story is finally a tale of hard-fought, scarred redemption.

In Harrison's own mystical universe, he would no doubt have describe his life in terms of ying and yang, the chance encounters of spiritual elements and religious planes. And the musician would be fairly on target. His well-known generosity, patience, and religious zeal was equally balanced out in the ledger of life by stories of a rigid, often puritanical nature, philandering and rampant infidelity, questionable, often misguided creative and personal choices, and a penchant for drink and drugs.

His creative frustrations are legendary. His experiments in solo ventures were occasionally successful, his three-record opus *All Things Must Pass* being the prime example. But, just as often they were pretentious and undermined by his unshakable religious beliefs; *Extra Texture: Read All About It* and *Dark Horse*, being major offenders, are famous and infamous. Harrison's on-and-off love affair with stardom is alternately understandable and perplexing, as was the man himself.

Consequently, unlike many legendary performers who always seemed to make the right choices, George Harrison's career has not been universally praised. More than one observer of the pop-music scene has lamented Harrison as somebody not willing to take a chance, preferring to play it safe rather than creatively roll the dice. It has also been said that while he was an intregal part of the Beatles, he never reached discernible heights as a solo artist.

Oh, and lest we forget, George Harrison can be downright boring. In later years, puttering around his garden and playing the househusband were highlights of his life. And when he would get on his high horse about Indian religion, often with the fervor of a fire-and-brimstone preacher, even his closest friends had to stifle a yawn. There's nothing very "rock star" in those moments but they are truly a telling of George's basic humanity and his strident need to come across as normal.

And so the task at hand: To discover the real George Harrison in all his varying shades of light and dark. And it is not an easy life to put in order. Because George Harrison spent his entire life trying to hide from us, and, depending on how one addresses that elusive beast called Fame, he either failed miserably or succeeded to the nth degree.

Long before he became a part of history as a member of the Beatles, George Harrison, who once proclaimed, "I don't want to be famous, but I do want to be successful," was battling to satisfy his desire to be as free and individual as possible in a world that held conformity in high esteem. He pursued music as a soulful, creative expression, not as a way to achieve stardom and material goods. Even during the halcyon days of Beatlemania, Harrison, who admittedly took full advantage of the perks of rock stardom, would often stand out as a serious musician amid the mania.

He was regularly the object of teen-girl debate along the lines of "Who was the cutest Beatle?" and "Which Beatle would they most like to kiss?" But, for those who looked below the paper-thin veneer of hype, hucksterism, and just plain bullshit that passed for pop stardom in the 1960s, there were other, more important tags being hung on the young guitarist as well. The Quiet Beatle. The Serious Beatle. And, yes, even the Sad Beatle. While Lennon, McCartney, and Starr were often the willing foils for the foolishness of pop music's starmaking machinery, one often got the impression that Harrison was better than what was going on around him and would eventually aspire to something more important than merely being a member of the most popular band in the annals of pop-music history.

Not that George Harrison ever saw himself in larger-than-life terms. Although his life was occasionally marred by bouts of egomania, when his obstinance surrounding his religious pursuits threatened to consume him, the guitarist alternated between running to and away from stardom and, at all times, keeping his life in balance. He became adept at living a stealth life, running smoothly under the radar in the face of constant public scrutiny; surfacing, often painfully so, when his musical life demanded, but preferring to shun the spotlight in favor of solitude.

The broad strokes of George Harrison's personal and professional life have been chronicled elsewhere—but always in the context of a burgeoning whole. It was always George

Harrison as part of the Beatles. George Harrison as the guiding light behind Bangladesh. George Harrison as the linchpin in the resurgence of Indian mysticism as the hip, new religion for the Swinging Sixties. George Harrison has never been allowed to stand alone, observing the events that unfolded in front of him and unveiling the inner workings, the personal asides and anecdotes that have marked Harrison's checkered, but never less than interesting, life.

Behind Sad Eyes: The Life of George Harrison will take you to that place. The history will be there—the names, dates, and places. The voyage of discovery from his days in Liverpool, and his transformation from boy to man during those raucous nights in Hamburg. His struggles with stardom and the frustration of being regulated to playing second fiddle to Lennon and McCartney. The conflicts that would ultimately destroy friendships, the sadness when lovers and close friends betrayed him, and the battle between personal beliefs and public expectations that met on a collision course with Harrison in the middle.

Harrison dealt with the onset of old age, marked by a brush with mortality and the spectre of the Grim Reaper pulling up fast in his rearview mirror.

You've been here before. But, you've never been here this way.

Behind Sad Eyes: The Life of George Harrison will take you to a place you've never been before: into the life behind the sad eyes.

—Marc Shapiro, 2002

Behind
Sad
Eyes
The Life of
George Harrison

one **Get Your Ass Out of Here!**

George Harrison returned to the spotlight in 1997. But not in the way he would have liked or, doubtless, would have been comfortable with.

That year, it was disclosed that a deranged fan had been sending George death threats through the mail that reportedly said "good-bye George" and "time you went." Only after the man was arrested was it discovered that the letters had, in fact, been coming on a steady basis since 1996 and that most of them had been burned by George's staff before he had a chance to see them for fear of upsetting the—by that time—already security-crazed musician.

In July 1997, while puttering around in the garden of his mansion at Henley on Thames Oxfordshire, Harrison discovered a lump in his neck. He would subsequently undergo surgery to remove what would turn out to be a cancerous nodule, followed by a month of radiation treatments. Harrison, who confirmed that the cancer had been the result of an off-and-on pattern of cigarette smoking over the years, pronounced himself cancer-free following that treatment. In January 1998, Harrison checked into the Mayo Clinic in Rochester, Minnesota, for follow-up tests and would again confirm that he was cancer-free.

Harrison faced true terror on December 30, 1999, when the deranged thirty-three-year-old, Mike Abram, claiming he had been told by God to kill Harrison, broke into the ex-Beatle's home and stabbed the musician several times in the chest, hands, and fingers before his wife Olivia subdued the attacker by hitting him repeatedly with a metal poker.

"I vividly remember a deliberate thrust of the knife towards my chest," Harrison related in a written statement introduced during Abram's trial. "I felt my chest deflate and the flow of blood towards my mouth. I believed I had been fatally stabbed."

Olivia Harrison also remembered the night of terror during her trial testimony. "There was blood on the wall, blood on my hands, and I realized that we were going to be murdered."

Harrison's personal trials continued to command headlines when, in April 2001, he underwent lung cancer surgery. In the wake of that operation Harrison appeared gaunt and sickly in public appearances to promote the reissue of his solo album *All Things Must Pass*, leading to active speculation that he was near death. The musician issued an angry statement that he was, in fact, "active and feeling very well" and that he was "disappointed and disgusted" at the ill-founded reports of his pending death.

That George Harrison was forced into the spotlight because of personal travails is ironic, coming as it does from a man who has seemingly spent his entire life running from prying eyes. As always he was uncomfortable in front of the camera's glare and the reporter's notebook. He wished it would all go away.

The at large opinion was he wished he could go away. But his life and times had already been marked by the pronouncement that George Harrison could run but he could not hide for very long.

During his years with the Beatles, Harrison, who struck an introspective/inquisitive image with his angular features, wide eyes, dark bushy eyebrows, and often timid tight smile, was the one most uncomfortable with the accolades and the press interest. He would do the requisite interviews, albeit reluctantly. When he did speak, reporters instantly marked him the shy and withdrawn member of the Beatles who would never look you in the eye while speaking and always projected the image of deep thought or discomfort, even when presented with the most innocuous teen-heartthrob question.

But he was also notorious in those early years of the Beatles for lashing out, in uncharacteristic fits of temper, when he felt his privacy was being intruded upon. However, Harrison, when he has addressed his feelings during the Beatles' rise to stardom in the 1960s, would patiently couch his remarks in the fact that it was people's seriousness about the whole idea of stardom and celebrity, rather than his personality, that was off-putting.

"I've always been a firm believer in freedom and privacy," he acknowledged. "Treat it all too seriously and you can't help but go out of your mind."

Which was why, during the heyday of Beatlemania, Harrison hid his discomfort with the intrusions on his every thought with a quick wit, heavy on the double entendres and the snappy one-liner: playing as necessary the perfect comic relief, not so much for the benefit of others as for himself. Harrison was not dumb. He knew there was a game that had to be played. But as Harrison would readily admit in later years, he was also aware that it was all largely a sham.

"I enjoyed making the records," he conceded. "But I didn't like to be on TV and do the interviews that were necessary to promote it. There was a time when I actually hated all that."

But he would always put up a good front. Beatles manager Brian Epstein acknowledged at the time that it was the rare moment when George was anything but accommodating. "George has his moods, though I cannot recall any particular moments. All I know is that George is remarkably easy to be with."

Harrison's near-manic distaste for the public interest in his every move had, by the time the Beatles shut down the crazy—and, for George, the least musically rewarding—touring life in 1966, begun to turn him against the very group that had made him famous. The arguments, especially those with John Lennon and Paul McCartney, had become increasingly heated. More and more, George was longing for time away from the limelight and what had become the totally reprehensible process of being a pop star.

"It made me nervous, the whole magnitude of our fame," he admitted. "I wanted to stop touring after about 1965 because I was getting very nervous. They kept planning these ticker-tape parades and I was saying, 'I absolutely don't want to do that.' I didn't like the idea of being too popular."

His frustrations at not being more than a token songwriter in the band also fueled his anger. So did his increasingly serious view of life that often seemed to run at odds with the attitude of the rest of the group. John had already staked out the role of rock-and-roll rebel and was content to play it to the hilt. Paul, while serious about his songwriting, was rather frivolous and accommodating to the rigors of pop life. Ringo was basically the laid-back easygoing drummer who said yes to everything and could be counted on to be the pliable follower rather than a leader. George could never quite find his place.

Consequently, his growing fear of the spotlight and his weariness of performing was the main reason why the Beatles never played live again after 1966. In fact, the only reason the band performed their now famous *Let It Be* rooftop session was that George refused to perform in front of an audience. When he stormed out at one point in the Beatles' onerous *Let It Be* album sessions, after a bitter argument with Lennon and McCartney, in his mind his life with the Beatles was already over.

In his post–Beatles life, Harrison would dismiss any questions about his Beatles experience as "rubbish." He stated there was little in the Beatle experience that was satisfying, and that even the best thrill associated with celebrity soon got tiring.

"It was awful being on the front page of everyone's life, every day," said Harrison. "What an intrusion into our lives. Your own space, man, it's so important. That's why we were doomed because we didn't have any."

Harrison's post–Beatles output, including the chart-busting *All Things Must Pass* and the less-than-creatively-exhilarating *33⅓*, was marked by an infusion of ego, fueled now by his now obsession with Indian religion. But, if anything, his own personal triumphs succeeded only in pushing him deeper into a shell.

It also did not help that George was often feeling out-of-step with the prevailing state of pop music. Loud, angry rock and heavy metal had become the order of the day, as had, at the other end of the spectrum, soulless pop ballads. George steadfastly refused to bend to the current trends, often pushing aside suggestions that his music not be so religious and that he rock a little bit more. Unfortunately, his attitude only led to not-too-veiled suggestions that George was, in his late thirties, a dottering old relic who was well past being of any relevance other than as a piece of nostalgia.

George had also become a bit of a professional liability. Getting him to promote his own records was tough. In fact 1982's *Gone Troppo* literally died of lack of interest on Harrison's part. He saw his penchant for privacy as something totally necessary and ultimately tied to his own personal philosophy.

"These days I don't go out of my way to sell records," he related. "If people like it, they can buy it. I'll do what I can as honestly as I can. I could go out and become a superstar if I practiced a bit. But I don't really want to do that. I don't have to prove anything."

His seeming not to care in a commercial sense led to much conjecture among critics and observers that Harrison, for all his resentment of his Beatles days, was suffering some discomfort that the group had broken up when it did and that, for all his productivity in his solo life, he would never equal that popularity on his own. It began to manifest in an increasingly unkempt look and an growing reluctance to talk about the past. In later years, Harrison would admit that "during the seventies, I just sort of phased myself out of the limelight."

But Harrison would find much that held his interest toward the end of that decade. While commercially successful, based largely on his name rather than any endearing music, critics suddenly began to find nice things to say about his music, resulting in the albums *George Harrison* and *Somewhere in England* being his best-reviewed solo outings since *All Things Must Pass*. Harrison took a shine to stock-car racing and exercised his desire to be behind the scenes when he got into the film business as the co-founder of Handmade Films.

Consequently, Harrison began to loosen up. David Cheney, the owner of the pub Row Barge, near Harrison's Henley-on-Thames home, recently reported that Harrison has always been an unassuming and natural person "who would often pop down for a pint with friends." And, in 1977, Harrison popped into the Row Barge unannounced and entertained the astonished regulars with a live set. George Harrison was definitely showing signs of coming out of his shell.

Until John Lennon was shot in 1980.

Throughout the 1970s Harrison had often made light of the occasional threat from a crazed fan, but the death of Lennon suddenly put the musician in real fear for his life. For the next seven years Harrison retreated into his home, turning it into a literal fortress of surveillance cameras, razor wire–topped walls, and searchlights. A sign near the front gate of his home pictured nine flags representing the major nations of the world. Next to each was the equivalent of a NO TRESPASSING statement. After the U.S. flag was the statement *Get Your Ass Out of Here!*

"At times you flash on it, when people call your name from behind," said George not long after Lennon's death. "You don't know who's crackers and who isn't."

However, George was nothing less than kind to those he allowed into his personal and professional world. Keyboard player Billy Preston, who helped out on the Beatles' *Let It Be* sessions and whose solo album George co-produced, saw that side of him. "George is wonderful. George is very spiritual. He's a very loving and humble person. He's a very good friend and is like a brother to me."

Even Eric Clapton, who has admittedly engaged in an

extreme love-hate relationship with George which resulted in Clapton's stealing George's first wife, has only the kindest words. "I think the world of the man. He's adaptable for any situation. His wit and his humor are a great source of inspiration for anybody who knows him."

As befitting his reclusive nature, Harrison rarely ventured out in public, preferring to work in his garden, play with his child Dhani, and, occasionally, to make a rare appearance at a nearby pub. In 1987, on the strength of his hit album, *Cloud Nine*, the very Beatles inspired hit single "I've Got My Mind Set on You," and the opportunity to be part of a one-off supergroup called the Traveling Wilburys (which also featured Bob Dylan, Jeff Lynne, Tom Petty, and Roy Orbison), George temporarily came out of the shadows.

Once again the increased interest in Harrison put the musician on the defensive and he retreated into solitude and the life of a landed gentleman. He remained that way until 1995 when he made the fateful decision to finally face his demons and join the other surviving Beatles in producing a documentary film history of the Beatles called *Anthology*, which that would be followed in the year 2000 by a companion coffee table–sized book.

Longtime friend Michael Palin (of *Monty Python* fame) stated that Harrison participating in the *Anthology* projects was an important element in his coming back into the light. "I think in some ways he is just now getting used to being a Beatle. I think he's deciding now that he can't live locked away all the time."

George Harrison has never put any stock in the speculation surrounding his often reclusive nature that has been an intregal element of his life and times. And he laid it out in typical George Harrison simplicity:

"That's then and now's now," he said of his hiding from prying eyes. "I'm reasonably well balanced about it all and understand, in my own mind, why I'm doing it. Unfortunately it will make me a bit famous again, but just for a bit. Then I'll go back to being retired again."

two

Life During Wartime

The world was between wars in 1929.

Emotions were running high and chance encounters and whirlwind romances were the rule rather than the exception. And so when Harold Harrison, a merchant seaman on shore leave from his duty as a steward with the White Star Line, literally bumped into Louise French in an alley during a night on the town, it was the beginning of a fantasy-tinged old-time romance.

It was the classic case of opposites attracting. Harold was a clear-thinking, deliberate man who did not waste words. Louise was bright, spirited, and possessed of an outgoing personality. Louise was reluctant to accept Harold's subtle but persistent advances at first but eventually succumbed to Harold's quiet charms and enticing personality. The couple dated for a time before Harold returned to the sea. Harold and Louise corresponded regularly, their love deepening with each succeeding letter. They knew in their hearts that they had discovered their soul mates for life.

A year later, Harold once again returned from the sea and the couple were married in a civil ceremony at the Brownlow Hill registrar's office on May 20, 1930. The newlyweds moved into 12 Arnold Grove, Wavertree, a small terraced house on a quiet cul-de-sac in a working-class neighborhood that rented for ten shillings a week. It was not much, but for the newlyweds it was every bit a fairy-tale castle.

In a better time, Harold and Louise would have settled quietly and happily into domestic bliss, with Harold becoming the breadwinner and Louise the homemaker and the mother of the children that were certain to come. But times and the economy were tight and Harold still had a merchant navy obligation to contend with, and so, for the next six years, the young couple, barely out of their teens, would frequently spend long months apart; Harold on the high seas earning less than eight pounds a month plus tips (much of which he sent home to Louise), and Louise doing her best to keep the home fires burning, working in a grocery store for the princely sum of forty shillings a month.

Harold and Louise made the most of their time together, and despite the obstacles of time and distance, were anxious to start a family. And so it came to pass that they welcomed their first child, a daughter named Louise, in 1931. A second child, a son named Harold, was born in 1934.

By all accounts, Harold and Louise were wonderful doting parents who, despite the constant pressures of the times, made sure their children came first and that they never wanted for anything. Consequently Louise and Harold were none the worse for their father not being in their lives on a constant basis. But Harold had long ago tired of life at sea and missed the time away from his family and so when his tour of duty was up in 1936, Harold Harrison came home to 12 Arnold Grove for good. The Harrison household was now together. But the stability of a two-parent home would soon come up against the reality of a world constantly changing.

With war clouds once again gathering over Europe, the job market had taken a sudden and drastic downturn and Harold found himself happily at home but unhappily out of work. For the next fifteen months, the Harrison family lived off welfare assistance, twenty-three shillings a week, which went into the necessities of life, rent, food, and coal to heat the house during the winter months. These were trying times for the family but, in particular, Harold who was raised with the traditional values of a man providing for his family. He would daily make the rounds, inquiring about any kind of work and finding none. His ego took a terrific beating during those jobless months and it goes without saying that Harold and Louise would have their rows regarding money and how to spend what little they had. Things began to look up in 1937 when Harold landed a job as a bus conductor, moving up to the job of bus driver a year later.

World War Two finally arrived full-blown on the land. The Harrisons could count on being lulled to sleep almost nightly by the sounds of enemy aircraft overhead. They would gather around the radio and listen intently as Winston Churchill exhorted his people to be brave and stalwart in the face of Hitler and his nightmarish buzz bombs. Although they were dealing with shortages of food and the insanity of trying to make already tightly rationed staples stretch for a family of four, the Harrisons managed to get by.

A second son, Peter, was born in 1940. Finally, on February 25, 1943, a third son, christened George Harold Harrison, was born. Harold, who always prided himself on being a no-nonsense, unemotional type, nevertheless had his heart in his throat and a tear in his eye when he looked upon young George Harold Harrison for the first time.

"I couldn't get over it," Harrison would recall years later. "There he was, a miniature version of me. Oh no, I thought. We just couldn't be so alike."

Although the arrival of George Harrison was totally unexpected, despite the couple's traditional Catholic attitude toward birth control, he was definitely wanted and, while the Harrison's spread their love and attention equally among all their children, Harold and Louise sensed that their last child would be something special.

Indeed, from a very early age Harrison was the picture of independence and self-confidence. Before the age of three, he was regularly running errands for his mother to the nearby grocery store where he could be counted on to bring home everything Louise needed without the benefit of a list. Because of their closeness in age, George and Peter were literally inseparable and, when not running around in their backyard or indulging in boyish antics, they would often be found playing in the streets and engaging in group games with other neighborhood children.

Louise French, with no small sense of pride, would regularly describe George as the ideal child. "George was always full of fun," she explained. "He never caused any serious trouble and even the neighbors liked him a lot. He loved animals and I was very proud of the way that he liked to help people. George was always giving away his money to tramps and old people who needed it."

When George turned five, his parents attempted to enroll him in a religious primary school. Unfortunately, all the Catholic schools were full and the one Roman Catholic school they approached would not consider him until he turned six. But Harold and Louise knew their son was more than ready to begin his formal education and so they enrolled him in nearby Dovedale Primary, a state-run, nonreligious institution.

Of no overriding interest to the child was the fact that a much older boy, John Lennon, was also attending Dovedale Primary at the time.

During his time at Dovedale, George's innate intelligence, rather than any overriding dedication to academics, allowed him to maintain good grades. Despite his small stature, the youngster also proved himself quite the athlete when it came to playground games of soccer and street games of cricket. While too young to realize what he was doing, George had already begun to develop a sly sense of braggadocio, more bluff than ego, that would allow him to ingratiate himself into any childhood group or situation. George's parents saw that trait early on and would often joke that their youngest son had the makings of a politician.

Money continued to be an ongoing life challenge in the Harrison family but George was largely oblivious to the importance of a pound and was, even as a young child, generous to a fault. In later years, Harold Harrison would regale interviewers with tales of his then young son's budding philanthropy, citing one day when Louise took George to the cinema. On the way there, George spotted an old tramp lolling nearby. He insisted that his mother give him half a crown which he promptly delivered into the dirty hand of the tramp.

By 1949 the Harrison family had outgrown their small house on Arnold Grove and moved into a much larger residence in the nearby town of Speke. The home at 25 Upton Green was much roomier but the neighborhood itself was a mixture of what were considered "good" and "bad" elements and, in ensuing years, Louise would often complain about the vandalism committed on their property by some of the neighborhood's less desirable elements.

George's strong sense of independence would occasionally

run afoul of Dovedale Primary's strict code of conduct and, as George angrily recalled the punishment meted out by the teachers could be painful.

"When I was eight or nine years old, my teacher Mr. Lyons caned me and got me on the wrist. It was swollen and when I got home, I tried to hide it but my father saw it and the next day he came down to the school and Mr. Lyons was called out of the class and my dad 'stuck one' on him."

It became apparent early on that George had a strong sense of imagination and was inclined toward creating elaborately complex, fantastic tales that he would use to entertain friends and family. Harold, who in his own quiet way would always cater to his young son, brought home some hand puppets to ten-year-old George. From that point on, remembered Louise Harrison, "whenever we had visitors, he always insisted on giving a little show."

George's flights of fantasy and imagination were beginning to give Harold and Louise pause. England was strictly a class-conscious society in the 1940s, and it was the rare child of a blue-collar family that went on to higher education, let alone a job not requiring one to get his hands dirty. But in George, they were seeing other possibilities and the notion was definitely there that their youngest son might be the one to find his way out.

George successfully completed his grammar-school education at Dovedale Primary in 1953 and matriculated to nearby Liverpool Institute in 1954. George's feelings about formal education at this point in his life were mixed at best. But on his first day at Liverpool Institute they were completely dashed when, as George walked the halls, a much bigger boy leapt out from behind a doorway, jumped on his back, and challenged him to a fight. For George, the die had been cast.

"The worst thing was leaving junior school and going to

the big grammar school," he recalled. "That's when the darkness began and that's where my frustrations began to start.
The big school, Liverpool Institute, was a real pain in the
neck. I knew then that the teachers were not the type of
people to teach. The way they sent you out into the world
was miserable."

His anti-authoritarian feelings aside, George initially made
an attempt to play by the school's rules. He would attend class
on a regular basis, made a point of being attentive and, to his
parent's delight, could be found most nights cracking the
books. Louise Harrison would often marvel at the fact that
while her son was not fond of formal education, he was a
good student. George has often grudgingly acknowledged
that he was a good student in those Liverpool Institute days.

"But I don't know why I was because I didn't actually
grind away at the books. I did some studying but I didn't
spend five hours a night at the books. It just came easy to me.
I'd zip through everything."

However, by his early teens George had given up any pretense of interest in formal education, and his notion that the
education system set up in England was hell-bent on turning
bright young minds into submissive drones was now thoroughly ingrained.

"You would punch people just to get it out of your system," confessed George of his frustrations with formal education. "I didn't like school. I think it was awful, the worst
time of my life."

George began to rebel in a way that was in keeping with
the times. The black blazer, gray flannel trousers, and gray
school tie that passed for acceptable school dress at Liverpool
Institute disappeared, to be replaced by such typically outrageous outfits as a bright yellow coat, skintight pants, and blue
suede shoes. George also took to wearing his rapidly length-

ening hair in a slicked-back style. Teachers were outraged at George's defiant new look and attitude. His fellow students were alternately shocked and amused. George's parents were, not too typically, divided on what they considered a phase their youngest son was going through.

Harold Harrison was driven to distraction by his youngest son's antics. He had been brought up to embrace conformity and stability and, in George's acting-out, he saw his son heading down the road to failure. On the other hand, Louise Harrison, always the more liberal-thinking and free-spirited half of the couple, regarded her son's extreme dress and rebellious attitude as both harmless and a validation of his individuality.

George would often relate how he never had anything less than total support from his parents. "Perhaps most of all, they never discouraged me from anything I wanted to do. That was really the good thing about my mum and my dad."

In hindsight, George Harrison's acting-out may have been more than the typical youthful rebellion. George's early independence and self-assured nature had also bred an unhealthy sense of cynicism well beyond his years. His problems with formal education only succeeded in reinforcing a strong sense that life was not going to be fair, and that the only way the youngster was going to get through a world whose rigid philosophy was largely stacked against him was to insist on playing by his own rules. George Harrison, by his mid-teens, was already an angry young man whose desires and ambitions were beginning to seep to the surface.

But by the time George turned sixteen and was in his final year at Liverpool Institute, even he had to concede that he was pushing the boundaries of what his parents would tolerate. That George would continue to tell his parents how much he hated school should have been a sign that, academically, he was in trouble. But, for whatever reason, Harold and

Louise chose to ignore the signs of trouble, feeling that a boy of such obvious intelligence and spirit would always somehow find his way.

The reality was that, in his final year at Liverpool Institute, George was in danger of not graduating. His growing disinterest had resulted in his overall grades dropping to near the bottom of his class—due in large part to the fact that George was rarely showing up in class and, when he did, he would ignore the instructors and, instead, sketch drawings in a notebook. When not in class, George could usually be found in the back row of the local cinema, waiting out the hours in a midday matinee until he could safely go home without raising the suspicions of his parents.

But as the year went on, a letter was given to George to take home to his parents that outlined in detail his failure in school and said that, in order to be able to receive his General Certificate of Education (the British equivalent of a diploma), he would have to take a preliminary exam. The note further indicated that to take the exam, George would have to have passed at least three classes related to his chosen career. Not having a chosen career was the least of George's concerns. By virtue of failing every one of his classes, he could not even qualify to take the preliminary test.

George was so afraid of what his parents would think that he burned the letter and refused to discuss his problems at school with them. But, when the school administrators suggested that it might be better for George if he were held back and allowed to repeat his last year, his subterfuge came to the surface and he felt that he had no choice but to confess his problems to his parents.

Harold Harrison was particularly upset at his son's failure. Even his normally supportive mother made her disappointment well known. But as these arguments often played themselves out in the Harrison home, anger eventually simmered down to the reality that George was an academic failure and that the only alternative was a steady job.

George went into full-time employment kicking and screaming. He knew that his years in academia had prepared him for nothing but a dead-end, low-paying blue-collar job. But he felt in his gut that he was destined for something better. However, the sense of guilt he felt in disappointing his parents soon led him to compromise his goals, vague as they were, and to finally settle on a position as an apprentice electrician at Blackler's, a Liverpool department store, for the sum of £1.50 a week.

The job was boring and, to George's way of thinking, totally pointless. But while doing such mundane duties as cleaning Christmas lights and cleaning out the men's restroom, his mind would invariably wander to the end of the day . . .

When he could go home and pick up his guitar.

three

When He Was Fab

George had never expressed much interest in music. But Louise Harrison began to notice something when her son turned twelve in 1956. He would come home from school with his school workbooks covered obsessively with crude sketches of guitars. Unbeknownst to Harold and Louise Harrison, their son George was undergoing a change.

Like most preteens of that period, George had a surface attraction to the popular music of the time, which was a folk-blues-rock hybrid called skiffle. He was also aware of such reigning pop singers as Frankie Laine and Johnny Ray and was finding a lot to like in American rock-and-rollers Buddy Holly, Eddie Cochran, Little Richard, and Chuck Berry. To that point George had actually felt intimidated by the form and felt he was not grown-up enough to be an active participant, limiting his rock-and-roll life to gathering with a small circle of friends to play the latest 45 or to listen intently to that week's Top 40 radio playlist.

But all that changed when he discovered reigning skiffle superstar Lonnie Donegan. George was electrified by the simplicity of Donegan's music and the emotions it brought out in him. There was something primitive and overtly sexual in the music that went hand in hand with George's entering puberty. The music seemed to speak to the frustrations and desires George was experiencing. George may not even have the questions, but somehow, some way, Donegan's music was supplying the answers.

Louise recalled when her son first made his feelings known.

"One day he said to me, 'This boy at school's got a guitar he paid five pounds for but he'll let me have it for three pounds; will you buy it for me?' I said, 'All right, son, if you really want it.'"

George fingered that guitar for the first time and struck a snarling rock-star pose as he stared at himself in the mirror. The look was admittedly childish. But he also had to admit that the guitar felt good in his hands.

That first guitar, a beat-up acoustic whose neck was being held precariously to the main body by a screw, held George's interest for a few days until he accidentally pulled the screw out of the neck and could not get it back in. Frustrated, he put the pieces of the guitar in a cupboard and promptly forgot about it. Three months later George took the guitar out of the cupboard, got his older brother Pete to fix it for him and began to practice in earnest. And to fantasize about the possibilities that beat-up guitar represented.

"When I was a kid growing up, the guitar was the main thing that saved me from boredom. It was the only job I could think of that I wanted to do, which was playing guitar and being in a rock band."

The guitar became George's salvation from a world that had increasingly offered him little stimulation. But his by-now firmly entrenched aversion to formal instruction led him to attempt to teach himself to play. Unfortunately, after some weeks of practicing, George was frustrated at the lack of progress he was making and began to express his frustration to his mother.

" 'I'll never learn this,' he used to say," recalled Louise Harrison. "I said, 'You will, son, you will. Just keep at it.' "

Louise's encouragement, which would be with George through the often tumultuous years to follow, was extremely important. George was nothing if not flighty and probably would have dumped the instrument for something easier, albeit less rewarding, if his mother had not been there, urging him on to even the smallest accomplishments.

Encouraged by his mother, George did keep at it, practicing at all hours of the day and night, often until his fingers literally bled. Eventually the youngster began to master the first primary chords and to pick out simple, skiffle passages. George would occasionally play along with his older brother, Peter, who had been inspired to get his old guitar out of storage by watching George and, most often, could be found attempting to play along to his favorite pop records of the day.

"I'd study the way the words were written and sung, then I'd go over them myself," he said. "I bought a little book with all the chords. I couldn't make head nor tail of it but I forced my fingers to put out the right chords."

George threw himself into the rock-star dream as he sleep-walked through his years at Liverpool Institute. It was during this voyage of rock-and-roll discovery that George, during the long and dreary bus rides to and from school, made the acquaintance of an similarly inclined student named Paul McCartney. McCartney, a year ahead of George at Liverpool Institute, was also a budding guitar player who amazed the younger boy by doubling in trumpet. The boys spent many hours talking about music, bands, and girls and grew to be good friends who would often go off on holidays together.

Their mutual interest in guitar cemented their already solid relationship and would often result in Paul stopping by George's house where, at the encouragement of George's parents, they would practice their meager repertoire until all hours.

"We used to play on our own, not in any group, just listening to each other and pinching anything from any other lad who could do better."

In retrospect, however, the relationship between George and Paul hinged on much more than just their mutual interest in rock and roll. Paul saw a bravery and bravado in George's feisty and often aggressively rude nature. This was much in evidence one day when Paul introduced George to another friend of his. George took one look at the boy and promptly head-butted him to the ground. Once Paul recovered from his shocked surprise at the act, he angrily asked George why he did it. George muttered some nonsense about how he was testing the other boy's strength and that the fallen lad was not worthy of Paul's friendship. Paul did not believe it for a minute but admired the younger boy's brazenness, and let the incident pass.

This incident was typical of George into his middle teen years. The proverbial chip was always on his shoulder. So was the element of distrust. For George, every waking hour had become a battle of wills that he was determined to win at any cost.

George's rapidly expanding skills coincided with the increasing limitations of his three-pound wonder. He would regularly explain to his mother that he was having a hard time getting certain notes out of his now ragged instrument and hinted, not too subtlety, that it would be nice if he had another, newer instrument. Louise Harrison's response was, "Sure. I'll help you buy a new one."

Louise managed to scrape together thirty pounds and soon presented her son with a state-of-the-art acoustic guitar. George was grateful but also insistent that he would not accept charity . . . even from his mother. And so for the period of time it took to pay his mother back, George took a part-time job delivering raw meat for a local butcher shop.

George's emerging talents as a guitarist fueled his desire to play in a band and in front of a live audience. Skiffle was the music of the moment in London in the late 1950s and any bar, club, or legion hall worth its salt would always have a night or two set aside for a number of local bands to bring in a young, free-spending audience. George was convinced that despite never having played in a band before and not knowing any other musicians other than Paul and his brother Peter, that he was ready for his professional debut.

And so one day George wandered down to the nearby British Legion Club in Speke and convinced the owner that he had the hottest band in town and that they were worthy of an audition. George came home that evening with the good news. Needless to say Louise was thrilled at her young son's daring, but shocked at the corner he had painted himself into.

"I told him he must be daft," she remembered years later. "He hadn't even got a group. He said, don't worry, he'd get one."

George immediately recruited his brother Peter and his friend Arthur Kelly to join him in his projected three-guitar lineup. Two other friends, whose names long ago slipped from George's memory, were added on tea-chest bass and mouth organ. This impromptu group, christened the Rebels, put together what they felt was a comfortable but extremely brief set of two songs. George, his confidence overflowing, thought the Rebels were great. The rest of the band were not quite so sure.

On the night of the audition, perhaps feeling a last-minute attack of nerves, the band decided to sneak out of George's house, one by one, through George's backyard in an attempt to keep what they were doing from the neighbors. The Rebels arrived at the British Legion Club and ran through their entire ragtag set for the club owner, who was impressed. Then he dropped a bombshell on the unsuspecting band.

The headlining band for that night's show had unexpectedly not shown up and so the gig was theirs . . . if they were willing to play all night. George and the others looked at each other. They were ready. Fortunately, the club owner was not too picky about what they played and probably did not notice that they were playing their same two-song set over and over.

From all accounts, George Harrison's first-ever live performance was a success, short on any overwhelming talent but long on enthusiasm. George would later relate that his first brush with the stage was a mixture of fright and excitement and that it was something he would never forget. Even more exciting was that the club owner happily paid them the headliner's fee, ten bob per person, at the end of the night.

"We thought we made a pretty good sound," said George in looking back on the Rebels' performance. "But so did about four million other groups."

The Rebels would never perform again but George became a regular on the Liverpool skiffle circuit and would regularly sit in with a number of local bands. Despite his growing reputation as a guitarist who played with passion and no amount of soul, the musically confident George, as a thirteen-year-old with no small amount of normal teen insecurities, felt he was not up to snuff. He would regularly lament to his mother, and occasionally Paul, that he was not that good a player and that just about everybody he played with was so much better than he was. But his shaky confidence did not dissuade him from continuing to play and grow as a musician.

In the meantime Paul, who had grown into quite the accomplished rock-and-roller in his own right, had hooked up with a local skiffle band in July 1957, the Quarrymen Skiffle Group, a revolving group of musicians headed up by a college student named John Lennon. With Paul's skills, as well as Lennon's determination that the band should evolve from skiffle to rock, the Quarrymen Skiffle Group would rise to the top of the semi-pro skiffle circuit in and around Liverpool.

Paul would regularly entertain George with tales of playing in the Quarrymen and suggested that he come around to their gigs. Finally, early in February 1958, fourteen-year-old George screwed up the courage to go to the Wilson Hall at Garston and watch the band play. George was immediately impressed with the much older Lennon's tough-guy attitude and trendy dress. And Paul in a live setting was something to behold.

After the show, Paul introduced George to John. There ensued the tentative dance in which the pair talked guitars and music. John was immediately attracted to the fact that George's influences favored rock, a direction John was trying hard to take the band in the face of what he considered the looming end of skiffle as a popular form.

At the time George and Paul, still at Liverpool Institute, were part of an informal group of student musicians who would get together in a room during their lunch break to jam on the latest rock-and-roll hits. John, at the nearby Arts College, began to come by and join the informal jam. He was impressed that George, his insecurities aside, knew a lot more chords and rock progressions than the current lineup of guitarists drifting in and out of John's band. But while musically George was just what John was looking for, his extreme youth and the sensed attitude of hero worship directed at him by George had John worried.

"I couldn't be bothered with George when he first came around," recalled John of their earliest encounter. "George's relationship with me was one of a young follower and an older guy. He was like a disciple of mine when we started. He used to follow me and my first girlfriend [and later his first wife] Cynthia around wherever we went. We'd come out of school and he'd be hovering around."

Eventually George's ability on guitar, and in particular his ability to play some sterling guitar lines on the then popular rock tune "Raunchy" during an impromptu audition in the back of a bus, and the pure insistence that saw him showing up at every Quarrymen rehearsal and gig, eventually wore John down and, by early March of 1958, he invited George to join the group. With the nucleus of John, Paul, and George and a revolving door of drummers, the Quarrymen broke away from the skiffle crowd and became a full-on rock-and-roll band.

It was also during 1958 that fifteen-year-old George Harrison fell in love for the first time, with a bright and wildly attractive girl named Ruth Morrison. To that point, George had talked a good game when discussing girls with his male friends and had been mildly flirtatious with the schoolgirls that had crossed his path. But music had been his overriding love to the exclusion of a romantic relationship. Until Ruth came along. Theirs was the classic teen romance: totally chaste with a lot of hand-holding and kissing but nothing else. At age fifteen, George was still a virgin and inclined to remain that way.

True to John's prediction, by 1959, the skiffle phenomenon had flamed out, to be replaced by a growing rock movement, typified by the so-called Beat circuit of fifties rock and blues bands plying their trade in a number of primarily low-paying jobs at a variety of clubs. George was still living at home and barely giving school a second thought. By the end of the year, he was out of school and struggling through his job at Blackler's out of a sense of guilt at disappointing his parents with his academic failure. The band rehearsed in an informal circuit that took in the homes of John, Paul, and George.

Through constant gigs in clubs and ballrooms, George was finding himself coming into his own as a guitarist. His leads became sharper and more passionate. His rhythm changes were constant and innovative. And, on the rare occasion when John and Paul relinquished the microphone, it became evident that George had a better-than-average singing voice. Another distinct advantage in having George in the band was that his boyish good looks (in conjunction with Paul's, of course) were drawing an ever-increasing number of single ladies to their appearances.

The Beat club circuit was a real grind. Most nights George and his mates could count on little more than a pound each for a full night's work. The club owners were notorious for not paying if a band went on late or came off too early or violated any number of myriad and arbitrary rules. Some nights the best they could hope for was a soda and a plate of beans for their efforts. But George would readily admit that he was enjoying the life of a semi-professional musician, despite the fact that he was dog-tired most of the time.

"We loved it like mad when we were first starting out," reflected George. "because all we ever wanted was to go around Liverpool and be cute and popular, play our guitars and not have to work."

Although John was the de facto leader of the Quarrymen, and all the early attempts at songwriting were Lennon–McCartney compositions, George had quickly emerged as the best guitar player in the group and both John and Paul would concede in later years that they were constantly practicing just to keep up. It went without saying that George was the element that the Quarrymen needed to break in to the big time.

One such opportunity came in 1959 when Carroll Levis, better known in London at the time as "Mr. Star-Maker," would be coming to Manchester to audition local talent for his *Carroll Levis Discoveries* television show. They were excited at the opportunity of making it to television and stardom but also a little concerned that losing under the name of the Quarrymen would be a blight against their local reputation. And so they decided to go under the moniker of "Johnny and the Moondogs" for the audition.

On the day of the audition, George was visibly nervous, sitting quietly and strumming his guitar while making mindless small talk with John and Paul as they waited to go on. According to the group members' collective memories, their set, with John on lead vocals and George and Paul laying down a deft guitar backing, went down fairly well and they received quite a bit of applause. At the end of the auditions, each band was required to return to the stage, play a few bars of their song again, and receive a final round of applause whose intensity would determine the winner.

Unfortunately, the show was running late and they were

about to miss the last train back to Liverpool. Sadly, they made the decision to get on the train and not return to the stage.

Although the Quarrymen continued to be a top draw throughout 1959, there were those inevitable periods where they were not working on a regular basis. George could not handle the downtime and took to moonlighting in another band, the Les Stewart Quartet. Through his association with that group, George became aware of a new club, called the Casbah, that was about to open its doors to live music. The Les Stewart Quartet was originally slated to open the club. But when an internal blow-up within the band derailed the Les Stewart Quartet, George volunteered the Quarrymen for the gig. The band's growing reputation preceded them and when word got around that the Quarrymen would be playing, more than three hundred people showed up for the August 29, 1959, opening. The band would be the closest thing to a house band at the Casbah for two months and would return for sporadic appearances during the early 1960s.

With George's musicianship as a driving force, the Quarrymen had turned totally to rock and roll. To fill out the sound, an art-school chum of John's, Stu Sutcliffe, was recruited and quickly taught how to play bass.

For George these were heady times. He was an adrenaline junkie, living on little sleep, questionable food, and an all-encompassing drive to play music. Being in it for the adventure, George was going through the expected emotional ups and downs of youth, complicated by the pressures of rising stardom. During this period he would occasionally confide to his parents that it was all getting to be too much and that they should all just run away and hide somewhere. To their credit, Harold and Louise Harrison, now fully behind their son's musical ambitions, would constantly encourage their son to stick with it.

And George would admit, when things were beginning to take off, that rock and roll was really a good job. "Money, travel, chicks, nice threads. There's a great deal to be said for playing rock and roll."

The evolution of the band continued. The band began putting their meager earnings towards amps and electric guitars. Their feeling that the name the Quarrymen was now too dated and quaint was followed by a suggestion of short-lived names that included the Rainbows and Johnny and the Rainbows. Eventually John came to rehearsals one day with the suggestion of the Beatles, taking his cue from the Crickets, Buddy Holly's backing band. But when the response was less than enthusiastic, the group agreed on the moniker the Silver Beatles.

On May 10, 1960, the newly named Silver Beatles landed their first real tour when they auditioned for rock-and-roll impresario Larry Parnes as the backing band for carpenter–turned–pop star Johnny Gentile on a two-week tour of Scotland. The band, with yet another fill-in drummer, won the audition and literally had a week to prepare to go on tour for the sum of eighteen pounds per person plus expenses.

For George, dropping the tedium of Blackler's for two weeks on the road in an admittedly third-rate tour went without question. George saw this low-level tour of dingy clubs and run-down teenage dance halls as the band's first glimmer of the possibility of making the big time. And it was with this attitude that George would revel in a tour that encompassed long drives, an accident that temporarily incapacitated their drummer, the way the rockers seduced impressionable young women, and the fine art of skipping out on a hotel bill.

Besides backing Gentile on his seven-song set, the Silver Beatles also performed an hour-long set of their own, made up primarily of rock-and-roll covers that included "Blue Suede Shoes," "Rock 'n' Roll Music," and "Long Tall Sally," and while all the band members had obviously grown into their rock-and-roll personas, it was George, whose stage presence had quickly caught up with his musical abilities, who shined.

The band's egos knew no bounds during the tour. Seeing their names and pictures on posters and receiving thunderous applause in hole-in-the-wall venues in towns like Inverness and Nairn was big-time for the headstrong young musicians.

Unfortunately, upon returning to Liverpool, the Silver Beatles ran headlong into a particularly dire dry spell. Despite glowing reports on the band's professionalism, Larry Parnes was unable to find another slot for the Silver Beatles. For a month after their return, they did little but sit around their respective homes and return to their dead-end jobs and unrewarding school lives. The mundane life at Blackler's and the sudden downturn in the band's fortunes hit George Harrison particularly hard.

"I was just about convinced that it was never going to happen," he confessed in looking back on those dark days. "It gave me great reason for concern. After all, the only other reasonable alternative was to just go out and find a real job."

After a time, jobs did start trickling in again but they were not the quality gigs the musicians were used to. One such date was as the backing band for a stripper named Janice as she took it all off to the accompaniment of the songs

"Moonglow" and "Ramrod." The Cavern Club, then one of the more popular local outlets for live jazz, offered the band a couple of dates on the condition that they only play jazz. For better or worse the band ignored those requests, often passed up to the stage by way of a note during their set, and eventually were not invited back. They were also managing a couple of dates a week at low-level bars and clubs where customers were more interested in drinking and fighting than anything the band had to say musically.

The future looked grim for George and the Silver Beatles in the summer of 1960. And George was dreading it.

four

Losing It in Hamburg

"We never did have a drummer," lamented George on the reason why he felt the Beatles had stagnated in the summer of 1960. "The drummers kept coming and going so, at that point, Paul started playing the drums."

Although the sight of Paul sitting behind a drum kit and banging away with reckless abandon was good for a few laughs, he was obviously not the answer to their problems.

Enter Pete Best, the son of the owner of the Casbah club, owner of his own drum kit, no professional experience, a recent school dropout with no prospects and willing to work for next to nothing.

The Beatles were leaving for Hamburg, Germany, in a matter of days. Pete Best would do.

Alan Williams, a manager-promotor who had acted as the middleman on the Silver Beatles' Scotland tour, had struck up a business relationship with German strip-show and brothel owner Bruno Koschmeider, who was looking to capitalize on the growing popularity of British rock groups. The initial experiment, involving the group Derry and the Seniors, had been successful and, early in August 1960, Koschmeider was looking for a second group to import into Hamburg to play nightly in a club called the Kaiserkeller which, under the club owner's direction, was attempting to convert from a strip club to a live-music dance club. The Beatles quickly worked Pete Best into the group and, after passing the audition, were told to pack and get ready to leave for Germany.

Harold and Louise Harrison had mixed emotions when their son burst through the door and announced that the band was going to Germany to play. Although only recently having turned seventeen, music had long since propelled him into the adult world and, short of still being a virgin, George had experienced late nights, alcohol, and all the temptations inherent in the entertainment world and survived them relatively unscathed. Harold and Louise had heard a lot of stories about what an evil, sinful place Hamburg was, and they were worried that George, going abroad for the first time, would be completely corrupted.

But on the day the Beatles piled into Alan Williams's mini-van for the trip to Hamburg, Louise packed George a tin of scones, made him promise to write often, and kissed her son good-bye.

George remembered next to nothing about the trip itself, except for a quick stopover in Holland in which John engaged in a minor bit of shoplifting. It was late evening when the Beatles arrived in Hamburg. And their first encounter with the city of Hamburg gave them a shudder. Dark, and with an instinctive dirty feel that seemed to hang from every building and entrance way, the city, a northern port, reeked of crime and corruption. However, once the initial anxieties passed, George could only perceive this as the beginning of a big adventure set to a rock-and-roll beat.

Bruno Koschmeider met the group and immediately took them around to the Kaiserkeller, a large, spacious club with a reasonable stage and an agreeable ambiance. The Beatles were encouraged.

Then Koschmeider dropped the bombshell: They would actually be working in the Indra, a much smaller and depressing strip club–turned–rock club. Their hearts sank further when they were led to their dressing room, which doubled as the men's restroom, and, later, to a dirty cellar stacked with bunk beds that backed up the Bambi Cinema which ran a nearly twenty-four-hour parade of soft-core pornography and less-than-classic westerns.

George and the others were too tired to be depressed and so they quickly unpacked and went to sleep. They awoke late the next day, to the sound of a movie playing in the cinema on the other side of the wall, set up their equipment, and, promptly at seven P.M. on August 17, 1960, began to play their first set in Hamburg.

The Beatles, used to playing forty-five-minute sets with reasonable time between shows, were shocked to discover that they would be required to play anywhere between six and eight hours a night with very little time off. Initially they were able to get through the night by repeating their patented set of fifties rock covers. But out of necessity they began to open up the set to include songs like Chuck Berry's "Too Much Monkey Business" and Carl Perkins's "Honey Don't." There was also a smattering of primitive Beatles originals that were beginning to be mixed into the set.

To avoid repeating songs too often, the Beatles' Indra Club sets began to feature songs that contained the opportunity for lengthy solos and jams. It was in these moments that the still very boyish looking George shined as a dexterous guitarist fully capable of providing crushing, jagged lead lines as well as thunderous rhythm passages. Through the sheer process of repetition and the necessity of improvisation, The Beatles were becoming a tighter, more professional sounding band.

"Our peak for playing live was in Hamburg," reflected George. "At the time, we weren't famous and people came to see us simply because of our music and the atmosphere we created. We got very tight as a band in those clubs. Playing such long hours we developed a big repertoire of our own songs but still played mainly old rock-and-roll tunes."

George Harrison's education did not stop at the music. The Beatles—whose nightly audience ran the gamut: drunken sailors, street thugs, prostitutes, and college students—soon fell into the rhythm of the city. They easily made friends with German locals and a smattering of expatriate college students, and were, in their off-hours, involved in drunken get-togethers, the use of uppers such as Preludin to get them through their marathon sets, and the cheap thrills of Hamburg's sordid red-light district.

Willing women were in plentiful supply to attend to the band's sexual desires, and they were particularly attracted to George's good looks. George, in the onslaught of temptations being thrown in his now willing path, finally let down his final inhibitions; and one night, after a particularly grueling eight-hour set and an equally crazed party, George Harrison, not too long after the Beatles had arrived in Hamburg, lost his virginity.

"My first shag was in Hamburg with John, Paul, and Pete watching," recalled George sheepishly. "We were in bunk beds and they really couldn't see anything because I was under the covers. But after I finished, they all applauded and cheered. At least they kept quiet while I was doing it."

As promised, George would regularly write home to let his parents know that everything was all right. Needless to say it was a sanitized version of what had become, for George, a willing descent into debauchery.

The first two months in Hamburg were taxing on a number of fronts. Although they'd picked up bits and pieces of German, the group was largely isolated. Their shows nightly turned into three-ring circuses in which wild drunks mounted the stage and attempted to sing along with the band. Their encores were usually a signal for waiters and fellow customers to roll passed-out drunks for any money left in their wallets. Throw in the lack of sleep, the nonstop partying, and being constantly in each other's company, and arguments inevitably broke out between the band members. One of the more amusing incidents happened one night in midset when George and John got into an angry shouting match right in the middle of a song. John laughingly remembered what happened next.

"We ended up getting real pissed about something and George threw some food at me. I said I would smash his face in for him. We had a shouting match onstage, but that was all. I never did anything."

That John would not lash out at George was a sign of how deeply the relationship between the younger and older musicians had grown. In John's eyes, George had grown in more ways than one. To his way of thinking, that translated into respect. For George, John's acknowledgment of him as a brother-in-arms signaled that he had left his youth and inexperience behind and was now a man of the world.

During their stay at the Indra, the Beatles had succeeded in transforming the club into a loud, raucous rock-and-roll club, and that ultimately proved to be their undoing. Neighbors were constantly complaining about the noise and, after a time, Bruno Koschmeider decided to close down the club.

But he was not about to let the Beatles out of their contract and so, in October, he moved the band to the Kaiserkeller.

Although they continued to work horrendous six- to eight-hour nights, the clientele—largely students, photographers, and artists—seemed more receptive to their music. Among them were commercial artist Klaus Voorman and his photographer girlfriend Astrid Kirchner. They had been electrified by the Beatles' performances at the Kaiserkeller and eventually befriended the English group and, in turn, introduced them to their student and artist friends. While all the Beatles were receptive to the friendship and, in fact, Astrid and Stu would eventually become romantically involved, this more intellectually inclined group were instantly attracted to George.

"We never thought about George's intelligence one way or another," recalled Astrid. "We knew he wasn't stupid, but he was just such a lovely young boy. He was so sweet and open about everything. I got on like a house afire with George."

The popularity of the Beatles in Hamburg was growing by leaps and bounds. They were the rare group that could draw on two distinctive and free-spending groups; the rowdy German tough drinkers and the intellectual student crowd. Their original six-week contract with Bruno Koschmeider had already been extended several times over the five months they had been in Germany and, with Christmas approaching, it was a safe bet that Bruno would want to renew again. But the Beatles had other ideas.

They had tired of Bruno's extreme bullying tactics and the squalid conditions they were forced to live in. Plus they also felt they should be playing in better clubs under better conditions. Through word of mouth, they discovered that the nearby Top Ten Club was a classier version of the Kaiser-keller. Subsequently they sought out the club owner, Peter Eckhorn, who was thrilled at the opportunity to sign the current hottest band in Hamburg to a contract. In contrast to Bruno, Eckhorn offered an increase in the sum they were making under their contract with Bruno and, of equal importance to the Beatles, cleaner living conditions.

The Beatles agreed and, one night late in November, they moved their equipment to the Top Ten and, with their contract with Bruno about to expire, felt no compunction about taking their act elsewhere. The vibe during their first show at the Top Ten was electric. Now they truly felt at home.

Twenty-four hours later there was a knock on the door of the Beatles' new living quarters. It was a squad of German police officers. And they were looking for George Harrison.

According to police accounts of the incident, an anonymous tip had been received that indicated George, only seventeen, was too young to be playing in adult clubs. Adding fuel to the situation was the fact that the Beatles, owing to Bruno's semi-legal way of doing business, had been brought into Germany without benefit of visas or work permits. The band members were convinced that Bruno had turned in George as revenge for their leaving his employ, but could do nothing about it. George would have to leave the country.

On November 21, 1960, Stu and Astrid drove George to the train station. George looked positively pathetic as he stood on the platform, carrying his battered guitar case and a duffel bag full of laundry, as he tearfully said good-bye. Astrid related, years later, that George looked totally deflated and felt himself a failure.

"I had to leave," recalled George of that sad day. "I had to go home on my own. I felt terrible."

The madness continued. Within a day after George's departure, Paul and Pete were accused of trying to burn down their former living quarters at Cinema Bambi, held in jail for three hours, and subsequently deported. Stu reluctantly left Astrid and returned to Liverpool, followed finally by John in early December 1960.

George had arrived home totally ashamed and defeated. All the big talk and predictions of stardom had led to complete failure and disillusionment. As the other members of the group dragged themselves back to Liverpool, their feelings were also quite negative. However, after a couple of weeks of licking their wounds and flirting, momentarily, with taking straight jobs, they once again took up their career.

On December 17, 1960, the Beatles played their first post-Hamburg show at the Cavern Club. The audience that night, many of whom had followed the band before their trip to Hamburg, were shocked at the change in the Beatles. The band was tighter-sounding and very much the high-powered showmen. George, perhaps feeling guilty and largely responsible for the band being thrown out of Germany, was a fireball on the stage of the Cavern Club, perhaps attempting on a not-too-subtle level to exorcise his own shame at the incident.

"What happened to me in Hamburg became basically one bad memory in an otherwise very groovy scene."

But many of the consequences of that "bad memory" would linger in George's mind forever. Hamburg was his first real taste of betrayal and it resulted in an ironic sense of cynicism, one much deeper than he had experienced in earlier years, beginning to fester in George's psyche. That it would never completely turn him into a distrustful personality was a testament to George's basic decency and good nature. His generosity over the years would become legendary but, in the days of Hamburg and the Cavern Club, it was measured in a number of little-known acts of kindness.

On one occasion, George drove up to the Cavern Club for a show and spotted two young girls close to tears as they pleaded with the doorman. George pulled him aside and asked what the problem was. When he was informed that they did not have enough money to get in, George smiled, pulled a pound note out of his pocket, handed it to the doorman and asked that he not let them know where the money came from.

The Beatles took the next step toward mass acceptance with a series of big dance-hall concerts, notably a breakout show at the Litherland Town Hall and the Grosvenor Hall, where audiences were driven to riot and the first critical superlatives began to appear in local reviews. History would look back on these shows as the first rumblings of Beatlemania. Through the early months of 1961, the Beatles appeared regularly at the Cavern Club, bolstering their popularity and finally laying to rest any doubts George and his parents had that he would indeed make a living playing guitar.

George Harrison turned eighteen in 1961 and the band celebrated by returning to Hamburg, this time with the proper work permits, for an extended stay at the Top Ten Club. Little had changed. They were still playing eight-hour sets. They were still drinking and popping pep pills. Stu had returned to the arms of Astrid and they were now making plans for marriage. Musically, the band could not have been tighter, and while John and Paul were becoming quite the songwriting combo, George's enthusiasm and occasional good ideas would often find their way into songwriting sessions.

"We performed like a gang of lunatics," recalled George of

that second trip to Hamburg. "We'd got echo mikes by this time and that used to add to the excitement. Honestly, if we had stuck to all the harmony songs, we'd have just about wrecked our voices. So we split it up and took turns to sing solo."

During their second trip to Hamburg, Tony Sheridan, another transplanted British singer, was the hottest star in Hamburg and a regular headliner at the Top Ten. So hot that he was eventually approached by local music impresario Bert Kaempfert to record an album. The Beatles saw this as an opportunity to get their ever-growing library of songs out, and arranged with Kaempfert to submit some of their original songs for consideration for the session. During the June 1961 sessions, in which they supported Tony Sheridan on a total of six songs (and at Kaempfert's suggestion went under the name "the Beats"), and recorded two songs as the Beatles, a rock-and-roll version of "My Bonnie Lies over the Ocean" entitled "My Bonnie" and a George Harrison–John Lennon song called "Cry for a Shadow."

Sheridan recalled in a 1994 interview that he sensed that the Beatles, collectively, were a top-notch band when he recorded with them. He felt that George in particular was a literal sponge during those sessions, soaking up the atmosphere and the studio vibe.

"George was very keen on learning anything he could," said Sheridan. "George was not looked upon by the others as being particularly good, although they liked his image and the way he stayed in the background. Of course he wanted to be more in the forefront but he felt he could only do it by improving his knowledge."

The Beatles' "My Bonnie" was released in Germany as a single in August 1961 and became an immediate sensation.

Copies of the single eventually made their way to England and into the hands of a record-shop owner named Brian Epstein.

By July 1961, the Beatles had completed their contract with the Top Ten and decided to once again return to Liverpool. The departure was bittersweet, in that band mate Stu Sutcliffe had decided to leave the band, marry Astrid, and become an artist. The Beatles returned to England, flush with the success of their second trip to Hamburg and riding a wave of positive press because of their continued prowess as live performers and the notoriety of their German single which had become an underground favorite in England.

At the end of the day, George's memories of Hamburg would be good ones. "We made quite a lot of friends over there. Friends as opposed to just fans or people who were curious enough to come along and hear us work."

In the wake of this upheaval, George found himself growing not only as a musician but as a person. He had rapidly outgrown his inherent shyness after Hamburg and was now more outgoing and, by association, quite the ladies' man. By the early 1960s, George was sexually active but, in line with the times, actual relationships were short.

A degree of arrogance was beginning to creep into his demeanor in keeping with that of a budding rock star. And George Harrison—by the time the curious record-store owner Brian Epstein had found the "My Bonnie" single, seen the band perform live at the Cavern Club, and signed them to a personal management deal on November 9, 1961—was most certainly that.

Brian Epstein liked to move fast. And "fast" when it came to the Beatles was landing them a recording contract. Brian used all his recording-industry contacts to full advantage, and on January 1, 1962, the Beatles piled into a van for a trip to London where they would audition for the A&R people at Decca Records.

They were scared to death. At Brian's suggestion, they did not perform any of their by-now long list of original compositions, but rather decided to do only standards. The audition, as typified by George's nervous vocal rendition of "The Sheik of Araby," was a disaster. Weeks later they would receive word that Decca had passed on the band.

The Beatles salved their disappointment by continuing their reign as top dogs at the Cavern Club and enjoyed their growing notoriety as full-fledged rock stars. It was during this period that George and the rest of the band began to feel the first intrusions that celebrity would ultimately visit on their private lives.

Fans began congregating outside the group's homes and it was getting to be impossible to leave without being swamped with autograph seekers and young girls screaming their names. George would often admit in years to come that he was emotionally divided on those early brushes with Beatlemania. On the one hand he loved the adulation. But in his mind there should, in an ideal world, be moments where he could go out for a quiet time with his mates or a girl without having to change clothes to disguise who he was or sneak out a back door in order to escape adoring fans.

George Harrison had discovered that, being a pop star, he could not have it both ways and he actively began to resent it.

There were hints that George may have been suffering some mild depression and no small amount of panic at going from relative unknown to being on the verge of stardom. Much of this discomfort could also be attributed to George's inclination to be a serious musician rather than what he considered the flimsy persona of a pop star. George at that time obviously was predisposed toward fame but was not completely fulfilled at the prospect of it. It would be a crisis of conscience that would follow him throughout the remainder of his life.

In April 1962, while their manager continued to try and get his charges a recording contract, the Beatles made their third trip to Hamburg, this time to appear at that city's most prestigious rock club, the Star Club. This final trip to Hamburg would have its tragic overtones as, on the day they were set to leave Liverpool for Hamburg, they received a telegram from Astrid saying that Stu Sutcliffe had died suddenly of an apparent brain hemorrhage.

It was a sad reunion in Germany, one that George took particularly hard. It was the first time anyone close to George had died. He was not quite sure how to react.

So he cried.

five

Phony Beatlemania

George was down at the rejection by Decca and the death of Stu. But the specter of success always seemed to be the tonic to bring his spirits up. The Beatles, while still unsigned, were now bringing in rather large sums of money and George was quick to spend it. His fondness for cars had resulted in numerous, often impulsive purchases. Clothes had always been important to him and now he could afford to wear the most trendy London fashions.

Needless to say, he had also become a massive celebrity in his neighborhood, the cliché of local boy makes good. And Louise, ever the proud mother, was reveling in George's success. She would greet fans who came around to their modest home in hopes of seeing George and chat them up about what was happening in her son's day. Occasionally she'd even bring out cookies for the fans. When fan mail arrived, as it was beginning to do in increasing quantities on a daily basis, Louise would dutifully go through each letter, often write a response herself, and suggest to her son which letters were deserving of a personal reply. Harold, while equally proud of his son's accomplishments, was more subdued in his praise; he let George know how he felt in passing father-and-son conversations but rarely let his emotions out to the degree that his wife did.

Following another series of headlining performances at the Cavern Club, Brian negotiated a new contract for their third series of appearances at the Star Club in Hamburg in April 1962. When he announced to the band members that they would each get eighty-five pounds a week, George was so happy that he would entertain anybody who would listen of his plans for his future riches.

His Hamburg friend Klaus recalled, "He felt he was going to make a lot of it [money]. He was going to buy a home and a swimming pool and then he'd buy a bus for his father."

There was more to George's attitude toward money than mere materialistic fantasy. Early in his association with the Beatles, Brian Epstein would recall being constantly peppered by George with detailed questions about how much the band was earning and what each share was. In later years, despite being represented by sound legal and financial advisors, George would regularly be all over the books with questions regarding concert revenues, record sales, and song royalties. The business side of what the Beatles were doing was of major importance to George, according to Brian.

In the meantime, Epstein, back in England, was continuing to marshal his forces in an attempt to land the Beatles a recording contract. Convinced the demo session that Decca had rejected was actually quite good, he sent a copy to his friend, producer George Martin at Parlophone Records. Martin was impressed, in particular with George's guitar playing, and offered them an audition. The Beatles returned from Hamburg, and on June 6, 1962, they performed a set for Martin—a series of songs including the originals "Love Me Do," "P.S. I Love You," "Ask Me Why," and "Hello Little Girl."

This audition was light-years ahead of their Decca fiasco. The band was tighter, much more polished, and, with an emphasis on original material, showed superior skills. Martin was also mentally ticking off the opportunities the Beatles would offer in the studio. He liked what he saw and heard. And he would get back to them.

While they awaited Martin's decision, the Beatles returned to a series of one-night stands that included the venues the Cavern Club, the Casbah, the Norwich Memorial Hall, the Hulme Hall Golf Club, and the Majestic Ballroom. It was all a calculated attempt to put money in the band's pockets and to impress record companies with their growing popularity. Finally, at the end of July 1962, Brian received a phone call from George Martin letting him know that he was ready to sign the Beatles and wanted them to go into the studio as soon as possible. John, Paul, and George were immediately told the good news.

They did not tell Pete Best. On August 16, Brian met with Pete and told him he was no longer in the band, claiming the rest of the band had decided they did not want him in the band anymore. His replacement would be Ringo Starr.

The reason for Pete's firing is still clouded in mystery, with various explanations being floated over the years. While the decision to ax Pete was ultimately a group decision, it was obvious that George—who behind the scenes had been complaining about Pete's drumming and his attitude—had been pushing Brian and George Martin to fire Pete and replace him with Ringo.

In the wake of Pete's firing, his many loyal fans verbally and physically accosted the three remaining Beatles at every opportunity. In one rather angry confrontation, George was punched in the eye.

For the first time, George had been cast in the uncharacteristic role of bad guy and he was uncomfortable with the idea, feeling it was not him, and, in what would become his typical response to uncomfortable situations, he denied any involvement in the firing of Pete Best.

George Martin took the Beatles into the studio on September 11, 1962, to record their first record. The A-side of the single was "Love Me Do," the B-side "P.S. I Love You." The record was released on October 4, 1962, and did respectable business in London and eventually crashed the Top Twenty. George remembered the first time he heard the record on the radio.

"I went shivery all over. I listened to some of the lead guitar work and couldn't believe it."

The Beatles returned to Hamburg for a fourth time before returning to England in November 1962 to record their second single, "Please Please Me," and just as quickly hopping a plane back to Hamburg for a fifth series of Hamburg shows. "Please Please Me" was released in January 1963 and went to number one the following month.

Although the Beatles came across primarily as a band, it was not surprising that individual members quickly began to stand out. It was also not surprising that John, the fiery, temperamental Beatle, and Paul, the cute Beatle, were getting most of the ink. But George was not to be left completely in the dust. With the aid of friend and journalist Derek Taylor, George struck a deal with the *London Daily Express* to "allegedly" write a weekly column, entitled "George's Column." While the reality was that George had only some input into the feature, usually suggesting a topic that Taylor would dutifully write, his six-month stint as a newspaper columnist did help him garner his share of notoriety.

The early months of 1963 were a literal blur of activity.

Their first headlining tour—a four-night stand in Scotland. Their first national tour of the continent, as the opening act for then reigning songstress Helen Shapiro. In February, they jumped off the Helen Shapiro tour and into the studio where they recorded the ten tracks for their debut album, *Please Please Me*, in just under ten hours. Then it was back on the road with the Helen Shapiro tour and immediately into a twenty-one-day U.K. tour supporting American stars Tommy Roe and Chris Montez.

George, now twenty, was experiencing stardom on a level that made his Hamburg experiences pale in comparison, and was quick to take advantage of the willing women, various substances, and the all-night parties that marked the tours. And although they were largely serving in a support capacity on tours, it became evident by the time *Please Please Me* was released in April 1963 that Beatlemania was in full bloom. That fame, at least for George, was already beginning to exact a price.

"After the initial excitement and thrill had worn off, I, for one, became depressed."

But George would readily admit that those thoughts never lasted long in the wake of their growing popularity. *Please Please Me* had gone to number one on the British charts and, although they were once again support group, for Roy Orbison on a May 1963 tour, a healthy black market for tickets to see the Beatles was already evident.

However, it would be September 1963 that would signal the official transformation of the Beatles from local British phenomenon to worldwide stars. That was the month they had the number one album in *Please Please Me*, a top-selling EP in "Twist and Shout" and the top-selling single in "She Loves You." Year-end tours in the U.K. and Sweden began to mirror the hysteria that had already taken hold in England.

Young girls were screaming and fainting, young boys were sporting Beatle haircuts, and the magazines and newspapers were proclaiming the Beatles full-fledged stars. Thousands of screaming fans would regularly meet their planes, and more elaborate ways of avoiding their adoring fans were constantly being created.

This was all thanks, in large measure, to the songwriting skills of Lennon and McCartney.

The duo had instinctively bonded in a creative sense which had resulted in literally dozens of commercial pop songs by the time *Please Please Me* was released. And with the pair constantly writing new material, it was next to impossible for the other members to try their hand. Ringo seemed quite content to play the drums and accept the accolades, but George was another matter. In recording sessions, he would often attempt to introduce his songs into the sessions or attempt to interject his ideas into a Lennon–McCartney piece. Of the latter, he would occasionally be acknowledged for his superior musicianship. Unfortunately, in the former he was usually rebuffed, which was a constant source of frustration to George, who looked on his songwriting as a cleansing process.

"To write a song helps to get rid of some subconscious burden," he once said. "Writing a song is like going to confession . . . to try and find out, to see who you are."

In September 1963, during a short break from touring and recording, George traveled to the United States for the first time to visit his sister Louise, who had married an American and moved to there in 1954. This was a happy time for George, with news of Beatlemania barely a whisper in America in 1963, he was able to walk the streets and eat at restaurants without being identified and mobbed. It would be the last time George Harrison would enjoy that kind of anonymity.

The Beatles' follow-up album, *With the Beatles*, would be the group's first million-selling album and their latest single, "I Want to Hold Your Hand," would hold the number one spot on the U.K. charts for four weeks while selling in excess of a million copies. The Beatles continued to tour England and Europe through the end of the year. To their way of thinking, in less than a year they had conquered Europe. Now it was time to set their sights on the ultimate goal . . .

Conquering the United States of America.

The States had traditionally been a tough nut to crack for British artists, and the streets of London were littered with those, such as Tommy Steele and Cliff Richard, who had tried and failed. Consequently the Beatles, and especially George, were mindful of possible failures across the pond.

"Apart from the odd singer, nobody had ever made it," he once explained. "So we definitely felt the pressure. But we knew we'd had sufficient success in Europe and Britain to have a bit of confidence."

Confidence coming, in large measure, because of Brian Epstein's late-1963 trip to America in which he laid the groundwork for the Beatles' first trip to America. During a protracted negotiating session with the producers of the influential TV variety show *The Ed Sullivan Show*, a deal was struck to have the group appear live on February 9, 16, and 23 of 1964. He also came to terms with concert promoter Sid Bernstein to book the Beatles into the prestigious Carnegie Hall for two shows on February 12. These two elements would form the backbone of the Beatles' first U.S. tour.

But the first U.S. tour would mean nothing if they were not flying into America on the wings of their first U.S. hit. After much hand-wringing over which of the Beatles' songs would be that all-important first release, it was decided that the pop anthem "I Want to Hold Your Hand" would be the most radio-friendly. George liked the idea that a rocking song, featuring his distinctive lead guitar work, would be the song to kick open the doors to America.

This was an attitude in George that was not uncommon. For while outwardly George was the perfect bandmate who would jump through fire if it helped the group, lurking below the surface was that self-centered streak that was always subconsciously thinking, *How is this going to benefit me?* This was not necessarily bad or good. It was just the way George's mind worked.

The group prepared for their invasion of America with a three-week series of concerts in France. Meant more as a warm-up for America, as well as a chance to strengthen their already iron hold in Europe, the Beatles were in for a rude awakening. The fans in France were not easy to please and, in fact, were largely sedate in the face of the band's first concert. There were no screaming mobs and the press was adding fuel to the Beatles' sudden insecurities in the face of a rumored British backlash that reportedly had fans jumping ship for the likes of the Dave Clark Five and the Rolling Stones.

Although they put up a good front in France, there was an air of apprehension on Pan Am Flight 101 as it winged its way across the Atlantic for a scheduled February 7 touchdown at John F. Kennedy Airport in New York. George, who was fighting a bad case of the flu during the flight, seemed particularly concerned.

"America's got everything," George was heard to say on the flight. "Why should they want us?"

While it was not discussed, privately Brian Epstein had real concerns that George's illness might force them to cancel the *Ed Sullivan Show* appearances and the Carnegie Hall concerts. Any fears that the Beatles might fail in America were quashed the moment the door to the airplane opened and the group saw thousands of screaming fans welcoming them with every element of Beatlemania they could possibly imagine. From the signs and buttons, to the fainting young girls.

The group deplaned and were led to an airport lounge where they were subjected to yet another round of often inane and repetitious questions. George, feeling sicker by the moment, did his best to entertain with his wisecracks and snappy repartee but, as Brian Epstein watched, he knew George was sinking fast. So much so that he called an early halt to the proceedings and whisked them off to the Plaza Hotel.

George barely made it to his room before collapsing into bed. His sister Louise, who had come in from her home in St. Louis to be with her brother, became his around-the-clock nurse. A doctor was called. With George laid up in bed and the fate of the *Ed Sullivan Show* appearances, as well as the other concert dates up in the air, the rest of the Beatles went to the studio on February 8 and ran through a rehearsal and a soundcheck, with their road manager standing in for George to keep up appearances. George made enough of a recovery that, on February 9, the day of the *Ed Sullivan* performance, he was well enough to play.

That night an estimated seventy-three million viewers watched as the Beatles ran through the songs "All My Loving," "Till There Was You," "She Loves You," "I Saw Her Standing There," and "I Want to Hold Your Hand." The reaction from the 728 audience members was vintage Beatlemania, with girls crying, screaming, and fainting. Outside, thousands of teenagers who could not get in were milling around for blocks around the theater.

Following their first appearance on *Ed Sullivan*, the Beatles traveled to Washington, D.C., where they made their U.S. concert debut at the Washington Coliseum in front of twenty thousand screaming fans who quite literally drowned out the band's set which was performed on a revolving stage. George would often relate that, for a band that had never played to more than two thousand people in Europe, playing in the middle of a sporting field in front of twenty thousand was a bit of a shock.

The February 12 shows at Carnegie Hall, the subsequent *Ed Sullivan Show* appearances, and their final concert of the tour in Miami, Florida, were literal mirror images of the responses in Washington, D.C. And although the Beatles' first contact with American audiences was a rousing success, nobody could have been happier than George when the Beatles got on a plane on February 21 for the flight back to London.

Turning twenty-one shortly after the conclusion of the U.S. tour, George was going through a transformation. He was relaxed and fulfilled as a musician and, at least outwardly, was comfortable with his celebrity. But there was also an edge of cynicism that was becoming increasingly angry. At one point in the flight home, those on the plane overheard an obviously exhausted George rail against what they had just gone through in America.

"How fucking stupid it all is," he reportedly said. "All that big hassle to make it, only to end up as performing fleas."

The Beatles' arrival at London's Heathrow Airport on February 22, 1964, was a national media event that was the lead story on major radio and television outlets. The members of the Beatles did the obligatory round of interviews and then disappeared for a few days' rest. George went home, only to find that Beatlemania had literally followed him to the doorstep of his parents' house.

Fans were outside Harold and Louise's front door all hours of the day and night and the crowds got so out-of-control that the local police had to be called regularly to break up the throng. Bags full of fan mail addressed to George were arriving daily. Louise, ever the supportive mother, had initially done her best to answer them, but by this time was overwhelmed with mail.

George had been looking forward to a few days of doing nothing and then a quick dash into the recording studio to record a handful of new songs including "Can't Buy Me Love." Facing this latest bout of adulation only succeeded in putting him in a dark mood. When asked by his family and close friends how the tour went, he continued to be somber and cynical in the face of his and the Beatles' growing notoriety. He complained bitterly about having to wear what he considered silly clothes, being chased by crazed fans, and having to sneak in and out of hotels in increasingly elaborate disguises. But what bothered George the most was that the U.S. tour, musically speaking, had been a complete and utter failure.

"We were cranking out music that no one could hear."

six

A Hard Day's Night

'**ve been grumpy at times because there were a lot of things we had to do collectively, as the Beatles, that didn't grab me personally that deeply."

Early in 1964, less than ten days after returning from their first American tour, the thing that was making George very unhappy was the movie *A Hard Day's Night*. Rock and roll and the movies seemed to be going hand in hand, especially when it came to British rock stars such as Tommy Steele and Cliff Richard. It was a way of maximizing their often all-too-brief time on top and it was often a segue into an acting career once the hits stopped coming.

It was a safe bet that Brian Epstein had all those things in mind when, while in America to set up the Beatles' first U.S. tour, he struck a deal with United Artists, to make a movie about and starring the Beatles. Originally titled *Beatlemania*, *A Hard Day's Night* would ultimately become, in director Richard Lester's hands, a slightly fictionalized documentary about the Beatles, complete with an even dozen of the Beatles' greatest hits. That the Beatles were not trained actors and the script, at the moment the six-week shoot began on March 2, 1964, was in varying degrees of disarray, only seemed to work to the film's largely improvisational strengths.

As tired as the group members were, the idea of making a movie did seem like a lark. Even George, whose mood could not have been more dark in the days following the tour, seemed amused by the idea of playing the fool in front of the camera. Unfortunately, while John, Paul, and Ringo seemed quite comfortable and natural in front of the camera, George, for all his dynamism onstage, did not appear to project any spark or personality in front of the camera. Consequently his early scenes in *A Hard Day's Night* are essentially walk-throughs with a look of boredom or disinterest on his face. Which is interesting because, years later, director Richard Lester, would proclaim that George was actually the best actor of the bunch.

In any case, George did not really care that much about what anyone thought of his acting talents. He was content to while away the endless hours on the set having a good laugh at what he felt was a boring and very undignified process for a musician to be going through. At the end of the day, George was too easily distracted.

Because by that time his mind was already fixed on something else.

Pattie Boyd was the epitome of swinging London in the 1960s. Her model-thin figure, long blonde hair, big blue eyes, and outgoing personality, all wrapped up in a miniskirt. It was no wonder that, on that first day of filming on *A Hard Day's Night*, George was immediately smitten. But, as Pattie would recall years later, the notoriously shy Beatle was reluctant to show it.

Pattie, a successful print and television commercial model who along with other young women was playing a small part in the film, had long been a fan of the Beatles and was in awe of being this close to them. During that first day of filming she screwed up her courage and introduced herself to them. Happily, she discovered them to be totally down-to-earth and friendly . . .

Except for George who, remembered Pattie, "hardly said hello." She felt at that time that George was shy or a bit of a snob. Or perhaps just plain not interested. Of the latter, there was much to support that theory. Because with so many willing women on the set at all times, the making of *A Hard Day's Night* was marked by instances when the women would sneak off to the trailers of John, Paul, George, or Ringo for quick sexual encounters. George was getting his fair share of that kind of attention from the first day and so, she speculated, he was already having his needs met.

However, during that first day of filming, Pattie was constantly aware that George was looking at her. Part of her was embarrassed and uncomfortable at his gaze but part of her was also quite flattered. At the end of that first day, Pattie approached the Beatles for their autographs. When she asked George, he signed his name and, under her name, he put seven kisses under it. Pattie sensed at that point that George might indeed be interested in her.

That George would express anything other than a sexual interest in a woman was news. He fully enjoyed women, liked to be around them and engage them in small talk. But he had never before expressed interest in anything remotely approaching a romantic relationship. This is what George Harrison was experiencing that day. If it was not love at first sight, it was pretty close.

George made his move at the end of that first day of filming. He went to her dressing room and asked Pattie if she would go out with him that night. Pattie said thanks but no thanks.

At the time Pattie was dating her steady boyfriend for two years and had no interest in being disloyal. George respected that and backed off, but during the ensuing week, Pattie's resolve began to dissolve in the face of George's good looks and quiet, sensitive demeanor. Sometime during that week, she went to her boyfriend and broke off their relationship. On the following Tuesday, George asked Pattie out again. She said yes.

George and Pattie were inseparable from that point on and the relationship moved at lightning speed. They became intimate almost immediately and had quickly brought each around to meet the other's families. George remembered that first date as a comfortable time in which they ate dinner and drove around London for hours talking about everything and nothing.

"I don't know if you could actually call it love at first sight," said George at the memory. "But by the end of the first week, I had already met her mum and three weeks later we were looking at houses together. So I guess you could definitely call us a couple."

And truth be known, George, at a relatively young age, had already sown enough wild oats to last a lifetime, and was, at least on a subconscious level, ready to settle down. In Pattie he saw his ideal mate in terms of looks and intelligence.

Pattie had experienced a small measure of celebrity as a model, but nothing could prepare her for the total intrusion into every aspect of her life that went along with being with a Beatle. Shortly after they became a couple, George and Pattie jetted off with John and his wife Cynthia for a quiet weekend in Ireland. She was shocked to find literally hundreds of reporters and photographers camped out in front of their hotel when they arrived.

It was all downhill for Pattie from there. During what was supposed to be a romantic weekend, Pattie discovered that their phones were tapped, they were constantly followed by the press when they tried to leave the hotel, and, finally, Pattie and Cynthia had to be smuggled out of the hotel in a laundry basket and driven back to the airport in a laundry van. Pattie quickly learned from the other Beatle women— Cynthia, Ringo's girlfriend (and soon-to-be wife) Maureen, and Paul's girlfriend Jane Asher—that being a Beatle wife or girlfriend meant an end to privacy. What she would never get used to was the letters that came as a consequence of her being with George.

"The letters upset me a lot. They were really nasty and said awful things. They always said they were really George's girlfriend and that I'd better leave him alone or they'd get me."

Pattie's discomfort only served to fuel George's own anger at his not having a moment's peace. To him it was all one big nuisance. "The fans, all shapes, all matter of humanity, were everywhere. We couldn't get in or out."

At the time he met Pattie, George had been sharing a flat in Mayfair with Ringo. But when they could not get the lease renewed because of the constant presence of fans around the building, George and Pattie moved into Whaddon House, Belgravia. But the fans and press quickly sniffed out their new home and the intrusions continued.

George finally found the home of his dreams and in July 1964 Pattie and George moved into a sprawling bungalow in Clairmont Road on the Fair Mile Estate near Esher. Although still near-manic in his obsession for privacy, George, perhaps naively, felt that the rows of trees and tall hedges surrounding the property would effectively shield him from prying eyes. But the rabid Beatle fans soon discovered his new residence and the problems with fans once again resurfaced.

On several occasions, George would return home from an arduous recording session, only to discover young girls looking through his windows. Once some zealous girls actually got into the house and stole a pair of his pajamas as a memento. But the worst incident, and one that finally pushed George to drastic measures, came the night George woke up to find two girls giggling under his bed. George had had enough. He installed electronically controlled gates, built up high walls around his residence, and took off the sign that identified it as the Harrison residence.

Although on the surface George and Pattie's relationship appeared headed for happily-ever-after, to those in the couple's inner circle, there were some obvious differences that had the potential for creating discord. Pattie was all wide-eyed and outgoing, eager to be a part of any scene and, once she got over the lack of privacy, happy to go along for the very public life that was the Beatles' universe. George, on the other hand, valued his privacy, was not the inveterate party-goer, and was often his happiest when shut up in his home studio with his music. He was beginning to show occasional glimpses of his somewhat puritanical, somewhat chauvinist demeanor. George was brought up in a traditional family where the father worked and the mother stayed home, kept the house and raised the children. While he did not come flat-out and demand that Pattie be barefoot and pregnant, there were early signs of manipulation in their relationship.

A prime example being the sudden increase in Pattie's modeling work shortly after the couple got together. George would not too subtly, and often indelicately, suggest to Pattie that she was only getting the offers because she was with him and that she should reject them out-of-hand. Pattie stubbornly refused to give up her work; and although in hindsight George was probably right about the reason she was getting a lot of work, it seemed obvious that he had an ulterior motive.

George's endless hours in his recording studio and music room had produced a number of songs that he felt would finally crack the stranglehold of songwriting held by John and Paul. But as the recording sessions on new Beatles singles and albums came and went, George's frustration continued as the often heated and combative song selection process saw his ideas and songs rejected in favor of the admittedly Midas commercial touch Lennon and McCartney, singularly and collectively, held.

John Lennon once gave a reason why George could not break through the songwriting wall in those early days. "He had been left out because he had not really been a songwriter until that point."

Consequently, while happy and somewhat settled in his personal life, George Harrison was not a happy camper by the time the Beatles began a European tour in June 1964 that would take them through September. In the midst of that tour, *A Hard Day's Night* opened in July to rave reviews in London.

While a by-now almost choreographed backdrop of Beatlemania continued to put the Beatles on the map as they blitzed Denmark, Amsterdam, Hong Kong, Australia, and New Zealand, the phenomenon of fame was becoming an increasingly tiresome and ultimately meaningless cross to bear. George felt particularly betrayed by the price celebrity had exacted on their ability as musicians.

"I was disappointed that we got so famous, because as

musicians, we were a really good band in the early days," he once explained. "The more fame that we got, the more the audience screamed and the more that we did just twenty or thirty minute sets of our latest singles, the musicianship kind of went out the window. We pigeonholed ourselves by the mania that was going on and the inability to perform for longer periods of time, because of the way it was."

A return twenty-six-date tour to the United States was a faceless blur of mammoth crowds, huge paydays, and a demoralizing series of huge baseball stadiums, endless limo rides, faceless hotels, and the increasingly annoying press. And, to George's recollection, individual incidents of that tour showed what happened when pop stardom collided with the dark side of real life.

A situation was discovered midway through the tour in which a mother had instructed her underage daughter to sneak into the hotel room of one of the Beatles, get in bed with them and then claim rape so that the band would be forced to pay a huge amount of money to keep this fabricated incident out of the press and the courts. There were also the occasional death threats, reportedly made by jealous boys whose girlfriends had thrown them over for the Beatles.

"Those tours of the United States were crazy. That first big American trip, when we arrived in San Francisco in 1965, they wanted to give us a ticker-tape parade and all I could think of was the Kennedy assassination and I remember saying no, no, no. In Chicago they drove us through the ghettos in limos right after the black riots. In Montreal, they burned the British flag and Ringo received a death threat. In Los Angeles, some jealous boyfriends of some girls we met shot at our plane as we were leaving Los Angeles."

Beatle records were selling in the millions. Concerts were

selling out in minutes. Financially each member of the group was set for life. But as celebrity and fame continued to shove them forward at lightning speed, George Harrison was slowly spiraling down into boredom and numbness.

Nineteen sixty-five was shaping up as more of the same as the Beatles, perhaps feeling the inevitable paranoia that their time was running out, were playing the total mercenaries. They said yes to every offer. Which meant more albums, nonstop touring in America, the United Kingdom, and Europe. But amid the chaos, George was finding 1965 a breakthrough year on a number of fronts.

In February 1965, the Beatles began work on their second film, *Help!*, according to the Beatles, much inferior to *A Hard Day's Night*—a cartoonish romp replete with the requisite amount of mugging and music. Among the madness of *Help!* was a sequence in which a group of Indian musicians attempt to pick out Beatles songs on their instruments, which featured the sitar.

George was fascinated with the outrageous shape of the sitar and the haunting, otherworldly sound it made. So much so that he sent an assistant to a nearby shop to buy him one. When the instrument arrived, George sat down with the bemused group of musicians and attempted to play along with them. It would be the beginning of a lifelong infatuation with all things Indian.

George's life experience would take a giant leap that year when, while at a party with Pattie, John, and Cynthia, he took LSD for the first time. To that point, George had indulged in soft drugs, marijuana, and hashish, along with a rather consistent drinking habit. The group's first experience with the psychedelic drug had all the makings of a bad trip that included frightening moments of being chased around

London by the friend, who insisted on controlling every aspect of their first LSD experience; stopping off at a couple of clubs where the group got a surreal rush that produced the expected colors and melting scenery; and, by the end of the night, pure enlightenment for George.

"For me it was like a flash," he once said of that experience. "It just opened up something inside of me, and I realized a lot of heavy things. From that moment on, I wanted to have that depth and clarity of perception all the time."

George's persistence in presenting his songs to the band finally began to gather some substantial victories. On the *Help!* soundtrack, George contributed the songs "I Need You" and "You Like Me Too Much." On the 1965 album *Rubber Soul*, he managed to get "Think for Yourself" and the very mature (by George's songwriting standards) "If I Needed Someone" on the record. Nineteen sixty-five's *Revolver* contained the George Harrison compositions "Taxman," "Love You Too," and "I Want to Tell You."

Revolver was also the album in which George made his first strides in Indian music by contributing the haunting sitar lines to the song "Norwegian Wood." The band was in the studio and, as the story goes, everybody was waiting for George to add the expected lead guitar lines to the piece. But George insisted that the nature of the song made it perfect for an alternative instrument and insisted that the sitar would be something new. John and Paul had to agree that it would make for a different Beatles sound and so gave George the go-ahead.

Following his introduction to the instrument in the film *Help!*, George had begun to dabble in the instrument, taking a few lessons in which he learned little more than how to hold the sitar and a few of the basics of playing. George knew enough, however, to add a lilting and primitively distinctive backing to the song.

George's arrival as a contributing songwriter at any level could be laid at the feet of several theories. The obvious one was that he had matured as a songwriter to a point where John and Paul had to take his contributions seriously. Another had it that Lennon and McCartney were so burned-out that they were more willing to listen to George's songs. The reality, according to John Lennon, was most likely a mixture of loyalty and a willingness to help George along.

"I remember the day he [George] called to ask me for help on "Taxman," one of his bigger songs. I threw in a few one-liners to help the song along because that's what he asked for. He came to me because he couldn't go to Paul because Paul wouldn't have helped him at that period. I didn't really want to help him. I thought, 'Oh no, don't tell me I have to work on George's stuff.' But because I loved him and didn't want to hurt him, when he called, I just sort of held my tongue and said okay."

The Beatles, singularly and collectively, were beginning to crumble psychologically in the face of nonstop activity. The tours and the expected mania had become predictable and only rewarding on a financial level. George's worst fears, that the band was becoming a parody of themselves and that their musical ambitions were being blunted by the fame, were becoming an ever-present reality. George would insist that the band, musically, had much more to offer but not necessarily in a pure pop arena. Essentially the others agreed but they also all agreed that it was hard to get off the ride at its highest peak.

His relationship with Pattie continued to be his refuge of peace and legitimate feeling in a professional life that had become increasingly tumultuous. Typical of his quiet, matter-of-fact personality, George proposed to Pattie in the car on the way to a Christmas party being given by Brian Epstein. Pattie related that they were driving along, listening to the radio when George calmly turned to her, said he loved her very much and said he wanted to get married.

"I think I just said yes or something like that. But inside, I was doing cartwheels."

George and Pattie were married in a small civil ceremony in London on January 21, 1966. The couple honeymooned in Barbados, spending their time swimming, water-skiing, and deep-sea fishing. Notoriously press-shy in his private life, George did an unexpected turnabout and willingly posed with his new bride for photographers who had tracked down the happy couple.

George and Pattie returned to London and got right back into the Beatles' wild ride. What would turn out to be the band's very last British concert was performed on May 1, 1966, in Wembley Stadium. Their latest single, "Paperback Writer," was high on the charts and, as they were preparing for their next U.S. tour, John was getting the band in all kinds of trouble by proclaiming that the Beatles were more popular than Jesus Christ. The response was instantaneous in America. There were public record-burnings, public denouncements from several quarters, and the kind of advance publicity the Beatles felt they did not need.

However, George gave those concerns only cursory interest. Because, mentally and emotionally, it appeared he was already on to what he felt were more important things. Whether it was because of his post-marriage settled nature, his increased use of LSD, or a combination of both, George had evolved into a more forthcoming and giving person who was now more trusting to new experiences and new people. And so it was in a more mellow state that George, during a party in June 1966, met legendary sitar master Ravi Shankar. Shankar found George to be "a straightforward, sweet young man" with an intense curiosity.

"From the moment we met, George was asking questions and I felt he was genuinely interested in Indian music and religion," revealed Shankar. "Then George expressed his desire to learn the sitar from me. I asked him if he could give time and total energy to work hard on it. He said he would do his best."

Shankar was impressed with his sincerity and the fact that he did not come across as the typical arrogant rock star. And so, in the next week, Shankar came to George's home.

"He showed me the basics," recalled George. "How to hold the sitar, how to sit in the correct position, how to wear the pick on your finger and how to begin playing."

At the end of the second lesson, Shankar suggested that, when his schedule permitted, George should come to India for a couple of months so that he could teach him in greater depth. George was looking forward to it.

Before they went to the States for the third time, the Beatles would do a swing through Japan and the Philippines. The usual parade of Beatlemania was balanced out by some unexpected thrills and chills that the group had not been prepared for. Prior to their appearances in Tokyo, an extremist student political group who felt rock-and-roll shows should not be staged in Japan, made numerous assassination threats against the Beatles which in turn led to a level of security that even the jaded band was not used to. Armed guards were present everywhere the Beatles went. Elevators would not stop on the floor of the hotel the Beatles were staying at unless a key was inserted by an armed guard.

Things only got worse in the Philippines when a purported snub by the group of a luncheon with President Ferdinand Marcos's wife, Imelda, resulted in more threats and government-organized street protests against them.

Putting an ironic postscript on their Far East ordeal, George laughingly stated, "We're going to have a couple of weeks to recuperate before we go and get beaten up by the Americans."

The Beatles arrived in Chicago, Illinois, on August 11, 1966, for the beginning of their fourteen-city tour. At a press conference before the first concert at the Chicago International Amphitheater, John apologized for his Jesus remarks. The tour itself was yet another exercise in shallow expectations, with the band playing a faceless series of outdoor sports stadiums in front of predictably riotous fans and through questionable sound systems.

"We got in a rut," said George of that last U.S. tour. "There was no satisfaction at all."

No one was happier than George when the Beatles finished the final date of the tour in San Francisco's Candlestick Park on August 29, 1966. Physically and emotionally spent, George settled into his seat of the group's chartered jet as it taxied down the San Francisco International Airport runway and into the skies, bound for London and home.

George signed deeply as the plane headed across the pond. "That's it, then," he said to nobody in particular. "I'm not a Beatle anymore."

seven

Time Out

George's proclamation was of the moment and nothing more. For while all the members of the Beatles had come to the same conclusion, that their touring days were over forever, they also all agreed that they had much more to give musically. But that would be after a much-needed rest.

John took the time off to do a small role in the film *How I Won the War*. Paul painted and did some music for the film *The Family Way*. Ringo worked on his home and had another child. In September 1966, George took Ravi Shankar up on his offer and, with Pattie, went to India to pursue his interest in the sitar.

At Shankar's suggestion, George grew a moustache and shortened his hair in an attempt to avoid the chaos of a Beatle in their midst. They also registered at the Taj Mahal Hotel under the name Mr. and Mrs. Sam Wells.

George immediately set to his lessons. True to his promise, he was diligent, as well as awkward, in those early days but proved to Shankar that he was serious about delving into the Indian universe. Shankar saw him as the ideal pupil, one willing to make any sacrifices to further his musical and spiritual education.

Things went well for a few days until George, confident

that his disguise had worked, ventured down to the hotel lobby to make a purchase. He was identified by the elevator attendant and soon the hotel was surrounded by hundreds of screaming boys and girls, necessitating a relocation to the province of Srinagar and to a houseboat where George's studies continued.

It was during this visit that George also began to discover Indian philosophy and religion. There was something in the lilting philosophy and simple goals of Krishna that appealed to George who, admittedly, when it came to religion, had been cast adrift for years.

"As soon as I read that [the book *Raja Yoga* by Swami Vivekananda], I thought, 'That's what I want to know!' They tried to bring me up as a Catholic, and for me it didn't deliver. But to read, 'Each soul is divine. The goal is to manifest that divinity' was very important for me."

George and Pattie returned to London in October 1966. The five weeks in India had turned their heads toward a better way of life. And as the Beatles prepared to go into the studio to record *Sgt. Pepper's Lonely Hearts Club Band*, it would be George, in so many subtle ways, who would guide the album.

George had immersed himself in Krishna philosophy, reading everything he could get his hands on and, as most converts will do, insisted on passing on every new spiritual and philosophical discovery to John, Paul, and Ringo. And so while it was no secret that the Beatles' increased use of drugs—and in particular George, whose smorgasbord of drugs included LSD, marijuana, hashish, and, mescaline—had a definite impact on the groundbreaking, heavily psychedelicized music of *Sgt. Pepper*. Reading between the lines, and the lyrics, especially the George Harrison–penned song "Within You, Without You," a strong case can be made for the convert-to-Krishna's influence on the often ethereal nature of the album.

George was easily the most enthusiastic supporter of the ideas being thrown around for the *Sgt. Pepper* album, feeling that the album would most certainly take the Beatles to a new creative place. "We've had four years doing what everybody else wanted us to do. Now we're doing what we want to do. Everything we've done so far has been rubbish. Other people may like what we've done, but it doesn't mean a thing to what we want to do now."

But George's creative victories during the *Sgt. Pepper* sessions were hard-fought. As usual there was the Lennon–McCartney roadblock to break through. As always, there was also producer George Martin's instincts to deal with. Martin, years later, recalled the struggle—one that he sadly recalled in later years had been a constant battle between George and himself.

"I am sorry to say that I did not help George much with his songwriting. His early attempts did not show much promise. I tended to go with the blokes who were delivering the goods. I did look at his new material with a slightly jaundiced eye. When he would bring a new song along to me, I would say to myself, 'I wonder if it's going to be any better than the last one?'"

Martin's predisposition to not liking George's songs carried over into the *Sgt. Pepper* sessions.

"The first song George brought up for consideration was 'Only a Northern Song.' I had to tell George that, as far as *Pepper* was concerned, I did not think his song would be good enough for what was shaping up as a really strong album. I suggested he come up with something a bit better. George was a bit bruised; it is never pleasant being rejected, even if you are friendly with the person who is doing the rejecting. When he came up with 'Within You, Without You,' it was a bit of a relief all around. I still didn't think of it as a great song. The tune struck me as being a little bit of a dirge. But I found what George wanted to do with the song fascinating."

With the completion of *Sgt. Pepper's Lonely Hearts Club Band*, George was now free to throw himself fully into the studies of Krishna and the search for what he was hoping would be the ideal spiritual guide. In the ensuing months, George would involve himself with numerous local gurus and experts in Indian religion in an attempt to find the right path to enlightenment. Inevitably he would come away disappointed. In the summer of 1967, he was encouraged by Paul to travel to San Francisco's Haight-Ashbury district, to observe the hippie movement where, Paul enthused, George would most certainly find inspiration.

George was excited at the possibilities of such an odyssey and, upon arrival at San Francisco International Airport, dropped a tab of LSD in preparation for what he felt would be a spiritual breakthrough. But, as his conspicuous limo moved through the fabled streets, George became increasingly depressed.

Rather than a psychedelic wonderland, Haight-Ashbury to his eyes was a slum. The hippies he had hoped to see, were in actuality lost, stoned, and disillusioned children. When George and his entourage stopped off at Golden Gate Park, he was immediately recognized by a crowd that surrounded him, handed him a guitar and insisted that he play something. When he politely refused, the flower children transformed into an angry mob. George and his people raced back to the limo with the crowd in hot pursuit. The mob surround the limo and rocked it back and forth before the limo eased its way through the crowd and out of the Haight.

So disappointed was George at his San Francisco experience that he immediately announced that he was giving up drugs forever. It was a promise he would not keep.

George persisted in his search for spiritual enlightenment, and slowly the rest of the Beatles, whose lack of strong religious beliefs made them ideal candidates for conversion, became disciples of the Krishna religion. Not long after returning from San Francisco, George discovered that Maharishi Mahesh Yogi, the guiding light in the suddenly hip Transcendental Meditation movement, would be giving a lecture in London on August 24, 1967, and insisted that John, Paul, and Ringo go along. That George could so easily guide the spiritual and free-thinking attitudes of the remaining Beatles came as no surprise to producer George Martin.

"George had something stronger than power," assessed Martin. "He had influence."

All were immediately transfixed by what the Maharishi had to say and, in a private meeting after the lecture, were invited to join him for a weekend of meditation in the New South Wales town of Bangor. Although the weekend of meditation and private audiences with Maharishi turned from serious to a carnival atmosphere when word leaked to the press that the Beatles were around, George and the others had effectively fallen under the spell of TM and were more than ready to take up Maharishi on the offer to travel to his private compound in Rishikesh, India, for a period of serious study.

George and Pattie were ready to go, but, as always, Beatles business had to be attended to first.

———————

The unexpected death of manager Brian Epstein on August 27, 1967, was a personal as well as professional blow. What his friendship and business acumen had meant to the Beatles was obvious. Of the latter, important decisions had to be made; the Beatles began to manage their own financial affairs for the first time, under a hastily formed business umbrella called Apple Publishing Limited.

During a post–*Sgt. Pepper* creative spurt, they also agreed to do a psychedelic rock odyssey film called *Magical Mystery Tour*, a road odyssey aboard a bus that had no script, no storyline, and which appeared on the surface to be nothing more than self-indulgence—as well as the recently completed series of songs that would also be released under the title *Magical Mystery Tour*. After securing the bus and shooting for two weeks under always chaotic conditions, an hour-long movie was cobbled together. *Magical Mystery Tour* made its debut on BBC Television on Christmas 1967 and was savaged by the critics.

The album, on the other hand, proved a solid follow-up to *Sgt. Pepper* that spawned quite a few future Beatles standards. George's contributions to the album were significant, with the rare group-credited composition "Flying" and the song "Blue Jay Way." By previous recording-session standards, the session for *Magical Mystery Tour* was a fairly easygoing affair, fueled by drugs, good vibes, and the relative lack of stress brought on by the fact that they no longer had to worry about immediately jumping out on the road.

After grieving the death of Brian Epstein, the rise and fall of the Beatles' creative fortunes held little interest for George at that point. For he was now fully ensconced in the philosophy of TM and the Maharishi. When he spoke, the conversation inevitably came around to his beliefs, and those privy to these conversations began to show some concern for the state of George's mental well-being. There was a fine line between simple religious fervor and and manic, unbridled belief.

And George, by the end of 1967, was showing signs he had crossed over that line.

George, Pattie, and the rest of the Beatles, their wives, lovers, and an all-star entourage that included actress Mia Farrow, Mike Love of the Beach Boys, and singer/songwriter Donovan, arrived at the New Delhi airport on February 16, 1968, to begin their advanced period of study and meditation with Maharishi. The inevitable press presence aside, George and the others quickly settled into an idyllic period of finding themselves spiritually. But not everybody took to the laid-back and often boring regimen. While John and George had thrown themselves totally into their surroundings and spiritual rebirth, Ringo soon became bored with it all and left after ten days. Paul also left not too long after, citing some pressing Apple business as an excuse.

George was finding the daily routine of meditation, lectures at the feet of Maharishi, strolls along the peaceful surroundings of the Rishikesh compound, and the tranquil times spent playing guitar and sitar to be a pleasurable experience, and no doubt would have stayed on much longer had not the real world suddenly intruded on paradise.

A rumor began circulating among the group of TM disciples that Maharishi had made overt sexual advances toward Mia Farrow. Rather than pass it off as a not-too-veiled lie intended to disrupt their spirit of harmony, the rumor began to take on a life of its own; especially after Mia Farrow suddenly left India without explanation. John recalled in later years that the story might have died of its own seeming absurdity if George had not, unexpectedly, decided to believe it.

"There was this big hullabaloo about him [the Maharishi] trying to rape Mia Farrow or somebody and attempting to get off with a few other women. When George started thinking it might be true, I thought, 'Well, it must be true because if George thinks it might be true then there's got to be something to it.' "

George and John immediately confronted Maharishi, who offered a stammering explanation that they did not buy for a minute. Within an hour George and John had packed and hailed a van to take them to the airport. Within thirty-six hours, they were back in their London homes.

The incident was memorable for its obvious insights to George's ever-changing personality and inherent, albeit quiet, strength of character. John was still the de facto leader of the Beatles but he knew enough to give way to George when it came to matters of religion and integrity. George's turning on the Maharishi, despite the fact that the Mia Farrow rumor was never confirmed, was indicative of how George often dealt with people. He was quick to trust but, when he perceived that he'd been crossed, he was also quick to burn that bridge—which was the case with Maharishi.

George and Pattie returned to a quiet life at their home in Esher. When not in London attending to Beatles business, George could be found at home, puttering around in his garden, entertaining friends and taking a lot of drugs, primarily LSD and hashish, as a psychedelic guide to his increasing fervor for Krishna. His associates were increasingly like-minded Krishna devotees who were drawn to

George's sincerity. Among them was an American convert named Syamasunder Das.

"George was always the one who was really sincere about trying to know God," related Das. "This wasn't just a casual sort of curious intellectual inquiry but rather a deep, deep longing for the truth."

And the truth eventually lead George Harrison to his first solo project, *Wonderwall*.

Through his by-now burgeoning reputation as somebody very much into Indian culture and philosophy, he was approached by the filmmakers of a lensed-in-India drama called *Wonderwall*, with the request that he write some background music for the film's soundtrack. Delighted at the opportunity to do something away from the Beatles, and anxious to try out his growing expertise with the sitar, he traveled to India in December 1967 where he wrote, arranged, and produced an entire album of tuneful, soothing, Indian-inspired music.

"There was this guy who directed the movie, Joe Massot," remembered George. "I don't know where I met him but he said he wanted me to do the music to this movie. I said, 'I don't know. I haven't got a guess of how to write music for a movie.' He said, 'Aw, we've got no budget for the music anyway, so whatever you give me, I'll have it.' "

Despite the intoxicating brew of having carte blanche, George was nervous with the idea but, armed with a stopwatch and a rudimentary notion of how to sync up snippets of music with scenes from the movie, he emerged from the recording studio with a soundtrack that satisfied the director and—unlike with the constant creative battles with Lennon and McCartney over songwriting space—his ego stroked.

The instrumental tracks were far from being commercial

but the album, *Wonderwall Music by George Harrison* did crack the Top 50 charts, based largely on the Beatles connection. Whatever the reason, George was quite pleased with what was essentially the first Beatles solo offering. And now he was actively dreaming of future challenges that would allow him to grow musically without the specter of the Beatles staring over his shoulder.

In November 1968 George, in his late twenties and showing a marked sense of maturity when it came to his music, went back to the United States for a visit with Bob Dylan. George and Dylan had been distant friends during the Beatles' touring days but to George's way of thinking, those meetings had been superficial and false. During this visit, all the barriers came down and the two musicians were able to deal with each other as people. During this visit, Dylan was generous and forthcoming in inviting George into his latest musical vision, sitting together for hours, swapping lyrics, chords, and ideas. George came away from his visit with Bob Dylan renewed, inspired, and anxious to make new and personal music away from the glare of the Beatles' spotlight.

The Beatles regrouped late in 1968 to record what would ultimately become the landmark *"White Album."* It quickly became evident that tensions were high. John and Paul were recently into new relationships and, particularly in the case of John, musical directions were becoming more divergent and even less Beatlelike than on the *Sgt. Pepper* album. Arguments became more heated. John was being particularly defiant in the face of his now more political and philosophical tone. Paul's patience in creative conflicts was surprisingly thin. Even Ringo, easily the most pliable personality in the band, quit the Beatles in frustration midway through the recording sessions although he would return a few days later. And, as was usually the case, George took his anger out with pen and paper and thus the song "Not Guilty," which would turn up years later on his self-titled solo album, was born.

"It was me getting pissed off at Lennon and McCartney for the grief I was catching during the making of the *White Album*," he recalled. "I said I wasn't guilty of getting in the way of their careers. I said I wasn't guilty of leading them astray in our all going to India to see the Maharishi. I was sticking up for myself and the song came off strong enough to be saved and utilized."

With his religious and philosophical attitudes now fully to the fore, George was able to slip below the radar of many of the problems inherent in recording the *White Album*, due in large part to the fact there was so much good material flowing from the individual members that the Beatles decided to make it a double album. Consequently George was a solid presence, with the songs "While My Guitar Gently Weeps" (featuring a contribution by his friend and like-minded guitarist Eric Clapton), "Piggies," "Long, Long, Long," and "Savoy Truffle."

Despite the overwhelming critical and commercial success of the *White Album*, the slow but steady disintegration of the Beatles as a cohesive unit was continuing. The follow-up album, the soundtrack for the animated movie *Yellow Submarine*, was done in fits and starts and more frequently, the individual members were not in the studio at the same time. To George, *Yellow Submarine* was more of a work project than anything to get excited about creatively, although he was amused at seeing his animated self play around in a trendy, truly psychedelic Pop Art world. The album did feature the George Harrison song "It's All Too Much" and the previously rejected *Sgt. Pepper* composition "Only a Northern Song."

However, George would continue to bemoan the fact that while his songwriting abilities had matured to a point where much of his work was competitive with that of John and Paul, he was still being relegated to the odd album cut or two, well away from the commercial spotlight. But rather than being combative and angry about what he considered some of his best work going by the wayside, by 1968 his more spiritual state had him waxing philosophical about the subject.

"Sometimes it's a matter of who pushes hardest, gets the most songs on an album," he said. "Then it's down to personalities. And more often, I just leave it until somebody would like to do one of my tunes."

On the surface, George and Pattie's marriage seemed happy. But deep down, some cracks were beginning to appear. George's attitude toward Pattie and marriage in general had become more rigid and controlling. George forbade Pattie to have a career and so she sadly agreed to give up her modeling career and soon became isolated in their home, becoming increasingly unfulfilled and stifled as the years progressed.

George and Pattie were almost frantic in their desire to start a family, but after years of trying Pattie still could not get pregnant. Privately George would often proclaim his embarrassment at being the only Beatle to not be a father. They went for fertility tests which indicated that, physically, nothing was wrong with either of them. Their frustration at being childless would often erupt into angry arguments. But the ever-gallant George would claim that the problem was his and not Pattie's.

A disintegrating marriage was not George's only problem in 1968. Although he had never graduated to hard drugs, psychedelics and hallucinogens had become a very real part of George's day-to-day routine—so much so, that even John, the most outrageous Beatle, would often comment on George's being "very heavy on acid."

George's religious pursuits also were creating a bit of concern in those around him. While continuing on with his Krishna agenda, George had discovered a new guru, Bhaktivededanta Swami, who was leading him even further into a rigid sense of belief. Consequently George was becoming increasingly intolerant of those whose beliefs were contrary to his, and was quick with the stern lecture and proselytizing when coming in contact with non-believers. Out of respect for George, nobody was laughing at him to his face, but more than one joke was being made at his expense, even by his closest friends.

On January 2, 1969, the members of the Beatles and another of George's growing circle of musician friends, keyboardist Billy Preston, got back together for what was at the time being called *"The 'Get Back' Project"* (which would ultimately be renamed *Let It Be*). Initially envisioned as a no-frills, back-to-their-roots album, the idea was to film the band at rehearsal for an upcoming television special. It was quite possibly the worst time for the Beatles to get back together.

John's relationship with Yoko Ono had, many believed, blunted his lyrical strengths, and the songs he was bringing to the *Get Back* sessions were considered, by Beatles standards, to be subpar. Adding to the growing division between John and the rest of the band was the fact that nobody liked Yoko, particularly George.

"I still can't believe the things George said to her," John

raged at the memory. "He told her that he'd heard from New York that she'd got a bad vibe. I should have smacked him in the mouth."

Paul's ego and seeming insensitivity to anybody but himself was also becoming another negative element within the group dynamic. Ringo, who had taken up acting in his time off, seemed more interested in reading scripts than drumming.

And then there was George.

The quiet Beatle continued to chafe at the idea of his songs and suggestions being discounted out-of-hand. He was also not comfortable with a camera recording what he considered to be their private moments in the studio. Like the others, George felt the sessions were long on hours and boredom, and short on production. Boredom became a constant companion. Tempers became heated. George was also bothered by the constant pressures of a Beatles reunion concert in conjunction with the *Get Back* album which already had been tentatively scheduled for the Roundhouse in London.

Most of George's anger was directed at Paul, who had become the leader of the *Get Back* sessions primarily because none of the others seemed too interested. In no time at all Paul had become a raving dictator. He had taken great pains to ignore John's suggestions and was particularly nasty to George. A day did not go by that he was not attacking George for what he considered mediocre playing and a bad attitude. This was a particularly telling blow to George's ego—because George's universe had begun to expand. He had been to different parts of the world, had played with a wide variety of musicians, and had been acknowledged as a talented musician in his own right. George seethed at what he considered Paul's slap in the face.

"Paul has shown a superior attitude toward me, musically, for years. In normal circumstances, I had not let his attitude bother me and, to get a peaceful life, I had always let him have his own way, even when this meant that songs which I had composed were not being recorded. When I had returned from the States, I was in a very happy frame of mind. But I quickly discovered that I was up against the same old Paul."

It all came to a head on January 10, 1969, when George exploded.

The incident, part of which was captured for posterity by the film crew, began with one of the seemingly endless creative arguments over song selection between Paul and George. Tempers flared, angry words were exchanged.

"Paul and I were trying to have an argument and the crew carried on filming and recording us. Anyway, after one of those first mornings, I couldn't stand it. I told Paul, 'I'll play whatever you want me to play. Or I won't play at all. Whatever it is that'll please you. I'll do it.' I decided this is it—it's not fun anymore; it's very unhappy being in this band; it's a lot of crap. Thank you, I'm leaving."

George stormed out of the studio, screaming that he would never come back. His anger once again resulted in a song, "Wah Wah." "I just got fed up with the bad vibes and that arguments with Paul were being put on film. I didn't care if it was the Beatles, I was getting out. Getting home in that pissed-off mood, I wrote that song. 'Wah Wah' was saying, 'You've given me a bloody headache.' "

But George soon realized that, from a strictly business viewpoint, it would be bad form to leave the band in the middle of an album, and his professional integrity eventually won out. A few days later George returned to the studio. But the damage had already been done.

Nearly a month of rehearsal tapes had resulted in nothing the band was happy with. George's growing concerns about performing live were a major consideration in the Beatles' canceling the Roundhouse concert. But as a compromise George was agreeable to the outlandish notion of the band performing an impromptu concert on the roof of the Apple building on January 30, 1970. The forty-two-minute concert was a cathartic moment for George, reflecting on simpler times before it all became too crazy.

Following the concert, the *Get Back* sessions became increasingly sporadic and unrewarding. Accusations flew with regularity and it was becoming evident that the Beatles could not be in the same room with each other long enough to create music. Friendships had been strained to the breaking point, to say the least. For all intents and purposes the *Get Back* album was, by the end of January, put on hold despite the fact the Beatles, usually not as a group, continued to play around with songs in the studio.

With lots of free time, George continued to study Krishna, puttering around in his garden, and indulging his ever-increasing penchant for psychedelic drugs. On March 12, 1969, Pattie was alone in their house in Esher when there was a knock on the door. Half a dozen members of the London drug squad, a couple of drug-sniffing dogs, and a warrant to search the Harrison home for drugs faced her. Pattie let the police in and, while they searched the house, called George at Apple headquarters. George alerted his lawyer and then raced to his house to find ten police cars and a paddy wagon surrounding his property.

Inside, George angrily confronted the officers who informed him that he was being charged with illegal possession of cannabis resin. George and Pattie were ushered out the door and toward the paddy wagon. Suddenly a paparazzo jumped out from behind some bushes and began snapping pictures of George in custody. George freaked out and charged after the cameraman, threatening to kill him. The terrified photographer dropped the camera and ran. George stomped the camera into the ground before being restrained by London's Finest and hustled off to jail, where he and Pattie were booked and subsequently released on bail. Nineteen days later, George and Pattie pleaded guilty to unlawful possession and were fined £250 each.

Unfortunately, the drug arrest was the last straw for George, who had become increasingly paranoid about the lack of privacy at his home at Esher. In the months that followed, George and Pattie would begin searching for a new home and eventually settled on a sprawling mansion in Henley-on-Thames.

But for all the turmoil in George's life, his dedication to Indian religion was providing him a cushion of serenity that allowed him to get through the less-than-positive moments in his life. He would make that abundantly clear to anyone who would listen.

"Through Hinduism I feel a better person. I just get happier and happier. I now feel for a fact that I am unlimited and I am now more in control of my own physical body."

Individually, the fiasco of the *Get Back* sessions continued to play on the consciences of the Beatles throughout 1969. Finally, in July 1969, they decided to put aside their personal and professional problems and get together again in an attempt to once again make lasting music. But while professionally things were moving in a more congenial atmosphere, personally the tensions continued to be present. Through all the upheaval that would result in *Abbey Road*, George managed a couple of personal creative high points.

The first song was "Something," written as a love song to Pattie. "I got the bit about 'Something in the way she moves' and the chord progression seemed to follow naturally. People tell me this is one of the best things I've ever written. It's very flattering."

The other was "Here Comes the Sun," a song written at Eric Clapton's house after a particularly trying day of dealing with business matters. "One day I stayed off [from business] and went to Eric's house because it's nice, with trees and things. The song came right out."

Although the Beatles would eventually return to *Get Back*, rename it *Let It Be*, and, with the aid of producer Phil Spector, turn what had originally been intended as an uncompromising raw album into the most orchestrated Beatles album ever made, the Beatles as a recording unit ended with *Abbey Road*.

George continued to hang around the periphery of the Beatles empire throughout the remainder of 1969. His growing fascination with new-age instrumentation, and in particular synthesizers, resulted in a totally avant-garde album of synthesized instrumental passages called *Electronic Sounds* that, while totally removed from the realm of commercial consideration, fueled the speculation that George, in his post-Beatles life, would be nothing if not musically adventuresome.

George has often had a good laugh at the simplicity with which *Electronic Sounds* came together. "All I did was get that very first Moog synthesizer, with the big patch unit and the keyboards that you could never tune, and I put a microphone into a tape machine. I recorded whatever came out."

He was also busy on the now active Apple Records front, signing and serving in various production, playing, and songwriting capacities. For the debut album of singer-songwriter

Jackie Lomax, George produced the album, played guitar on some cuts, and wrote the song "Sour Milk Sea." On the Billy Preston album *That's the Way God Planned It*, George produced. He also produced, arranged, and performed on the debut LP of the exotic Radha Krishna Temple, and wrote, produced, and played guitar on several tracks of the debut Apple release of singer Doris Troy. And finally, under the guise of L'Angelo Mysterioso (because he was contractually obligated not to use his own name when playing on artists who were not on the Beatles' label), he played guitar on the track "Never Tell Your Mother She's out of Tune" on Jack Bruce's album, *Songs for a Tailor*.

But as he would often explain, it was getting more and more uncomfortable to be even within whispering distance of anything Beatles. Although he would publicly proclaim that the much-publicized end to their working together was amicable, the reality was that George could not get far enough away from his former mates.

Growing personal and legal entanglements would bring an official end to the Beatles in 1970. But by that time George Harrison was already finally and completely on his own.

"Once the last Beatles album was finished, I was raring to go. I'd got so much music inside me that I was musically constipated. I feel as if all this is far behind me. It all seems so trivial, it doesn't matter anymore. What I am interested in now is finding out the answers to the real questions. The things that really matter in life."

eight

George's Blues

George Harrison and Eric Clapton had been friends since 1964 when the Beatles and Eric's band the Yardbirds would occasionally cross paths. But as in most cases, when it came to George and friendship, the two musicians saw through the egomania and bullshit of the rock-star life and found they shared a personal and creative soul.

Musically they were very much in sync. When George was creating the *Wonderwall* album, he rang up the guitarist, who was all too happy to hop over to India to lay down some bluesy licks. Likewise, when Clapton was short of inspiration on his trademark guitar ode "Badge," he gladly rang up George and traded his ideas for a co-songwriting credit.

Eric Clapton met Pattie Harrison at a concert in 1969. It was the last gasp of his group Cream's meteoric rise to stardom.

"I fell in love with her at first sight and it got heavier and heavier for me. I remember feeling a dreadful emptiness because I was certain I was never going to meet a woman quite that beautiful for myself."

However, Clapton, despite being a known womanizer and in the early stages of a slide into major hard-drug dependency as Cream evolved into the ill-fated and short-lived supergroup Blind Faith, felt early on that his friendship with

George outweighed any thoughts he might have had about stealing his best friend's wife. At least for the moment.

Truth be known, Pattie was in a fairly vulnerable state herself toward the end of 1969. Their continued inability to have children, as well as George's being dead-set against the notion of adoption, had begun to test the bonds of their love. So did George's by-now almost legendary adherence to Krishna; especially the more extreme tenets that forbade sex for pleasure. George continued to avoid undue publicity at all costs and, to his way of thinking, that attitude extended to his wife. Pattie was not allowed to work professionally or even to do charity work, lest it draw any kind of publicity to him. So, sadly, Pattie was often alone—and wishing she was not.

After the demise of Blind Faith in 1969, Eric Clapton was looking for a lower profile and part of that centered on his purchasing a home away from the hubbub of London, a home, coincidentally, quite near the Harrisons'. He was a frequent visitor and did his best to keep even any hint of interest in George's wife from being noticeable. It seemed to work initially, as neither George nor Pattie had an inkling of Eric's true feelings. Although, as perceptive as George had proved to be, it is well worth speculating that George *was* aware, took it as a harmless flirtation, and, most likely, as a stroke to his male ego that his woman could turn other men's heads.

Following the demise of the Beatles, George had been keeping himself busy with studio and production work but he began feeling the itch to perform live again, which he had not scratched since 1966 (the *Let It Be* show notwithstanding). On December 5, 1969, George and Pattie, along with the rest of the Beatles, went to London's Royal Albert Hall to see the all-star aggregation called Delaney and Bonnie and Friends. Delaney and Bonnie, who had a number of Top Ten hits in the mid-1960s with their hybrid mixing of soul, blues, country, and rhythm and blues, had added "and Friends" to a loosely knit touring company that picked up stellar musicians along the way. The lineup that rolled into London that night to begin what would be a two-month tour through England, Germany, and Sweden, contained Eric Clapton, Dave Mason, Bobby Whitlock, Billy Preston, Nicky Hopkins, Klaus Voorman, Rita Coolidge, and Jim Gordon.

Watching Delaney and Bonnie and Friends perform good old rock and roll in a jam-oriented, good-time family atmosphere magically transported George back to the time before the fame, when having a good blow was all that mattered. He was transfixed by the ease and the emotion of the music he was hearing. Despite nearing thirty, there was a little boy inside George Harrison that wanted that excitement again.

Delaney Bramlett recalled that he greeted the usual round of visitors backstage but was happily surprised to see the Beatles and an especially wide-eyed George.

"George just came backstage and we started talking and he said how much he liked the show and, all of a sudden, he asked, 'Can I do the tour with you?' I said, 'Sure, of course you can play.' He said, 'Well, can you pick me up at my house?' I said, 'Sure, but does anybody know how to get there?' Well, we had Klaus Voorman, Billy Preston, and a whole lot of other people in the band who knew where George lived so I said no problem."

That night, George made ready his gear and with Pattie's help packed some clothes. George was like a little boy as he excitedly prepared to leave. Patti put up a brave and encouraging front but, in reality, was upset that George would just up and leave her that way. Consequently Pattie could not hide her feelings the next morning when the bus carrying the band pulled up in front of George's home.

"We came by in our bus and there was all of George's gear sitting outside on the sidewalk," said Delaney. "I went up to the door and there was George, all ready to go, and insisting that they immediately load up his stuff. George went back into the house to get a couple of things as Pattie came to the doorway. I asked Pattie if she was okay with this and she said, 'Fine,' turned around, and walked back into the house. I don't think Pattie was okay with it. It sure didn't seem like she liked the idea very much."

Delaney reflected on the fact that the already rambunctious nature of the band and tour took on an even greater air of excitement when George stepped aboard.

"It was odd. I'm just a musician and a singer. I was definitely in awe of the Beatles. But George acted like he was basically in awe of me. It was basically two musicians getting together and liking what the other did. For me, he was just like one of the gang from day one."

But the musician acknowledged that George's presence caused a stir among even those musicians he had a long-standing relationship with. "They were definitely excited. The idea of having a Beatle on tour with us was definitely startling to everybody. But it didn't take more than overnight for everybody to become comfortable with everybody else."

The first concert with George in the band was a literal return to his roots as Delaney and Bonnie and Friends played to a sold-out crowd at the Liverpool Empire. George, perhaps suffering a bit of stage fright and/or rust, stayed mostly in the background but did venture forth at one point to say, "This brings back a lot of memories." But, by the next show,

George, at the encouragement of Delaney, began to step out front and take his solos.

"I would say, 'George, I want you to step on up here and take some solos.' He said, 'I will, but this is your show. I've had my time in the sun, this is yours.' I told him, 'I want you to be comfortable and take a solo once in a while.' So then he started stepping up. You can't imagine what it was like. I was playing guitar. Eric Clapton was playing guitar. George Harrison was playing guitar and Dave Mason was playing guitar. Nobody was getting in anybody's way. It was fantastic.

"He loosened up a lot after that first night," continued Delaney. "He really let his hair down. He'd be running around the stage like a crazy man."

It was also during this tour that George, at least temporarily, renounced the tenets of his religious beliefs and reverted back to his rock-and-roll ways with abandon.

Delaney laughingly recalled how shy-guy George suddenly turned into a party animal about midway through the "and Friends" tour. "He definitely got a little rambunctious about the middle of the tour. He would drink until it was dry. After every show, we'd have parties. We'd just go into bars, there would be three or four feet of beer on the floor, we'd have food fights and there would be a lot of destruction that we would end up paying for. In a couple of instances, we'd go to bars, they would be locked, and George would break the locks and we'd all rush in. The cops were called on us a few times but as soon as they saw it was George Harrison in the middle of this wild party, they would back off and the bar owner would usually say there was no problem. One night George got really crazy drunk and tore off the green velvet pants I was wearing and I ended up running down the street naked, chasing after the tour bus."

Given his isolation from domestic life, the speculation has run rampant for years that George used the occasion of the Delaney and Bonnie and Friends tour to cheat on Pattie with what Delaney described as "the thousands of groupies waiting for us to get back on the bus." But as far as Delaney could see, George remained faithful to Pattie.

"He could have gotten sex if he wanted. But no, he didn't. When we got to the hotels, everybody had separate rooms so I don't know what was going on at that point. But I don't think George was the type of guy to cheat on his wife. I think he was dearly in love with Pattie and so I don't think he had any desire to cheat on her."

According to Delaney, George adapted quite well to the unpredictable, jam-oriented nature of the tour. He would use his time on the tour bus to figure out what he would play on the next show so he would not get in anybody else's way. George's repertoire on the tour consisted of old rock and roll, usually a Carl Perkins song or two and, although Delaney said that George was free to play whatever he wanted, he never indicated a desire to play a Beatles song.

It also became clear during the tour that George, perhaps already looking forward to a more diverse musical future, would pick the brains of other musicians about styles of songwriting and playing. Delaney remembered how George approached him one night after a show in a dressing room with a musical question.

"George came over to me and said, 'You write a lot of gospel songs. I'd like to know what inspires you to do that.' And so I gave him my explanation. I told him, 'I get things from the Bible, from what a preacher may say, or just the feelings I felt toward God.' He said, 'Well, can you give me a "for instance"? How would you start?' So I grabbed my guitar and started playing the Chiffons melody from 'He's So Fine' and then sang the words, 'My sweet Lord / Oh, my Lord / Oh, my Lord / I just wanna be with you . . . ' George said okay. Then I said, 'Then you praise the Lord in your own way.' Rita and Bonnie were there and so I told them when we got to this one part to sing, 'Hallelujah.' They did. George said okay."

The tour concluded on a bizarre note at London's Lyceum Theatre where the band, including George, became a loosely configured, noisy Plastic Ono Band in support of John Lennon and Yoko Ono. Delaney observed that George and John got along quite well that night, indicating, at least at that point, that they were on good terms in the wake of the Beatles' breakup.

George was much in evidence on the live album that chronicled the tour, *Delaney and Bonnie and Friends on Tour.* But, owing to a contract that limited his playing only to acts on the Beatles' label, he once again found himself credited as "Mysterioso" on the album credits.

George returned to Pattie following the tour. Pattie was overjoyed to have him back and hoped against hope that his being on the road would, somehow, reignite the passion in their marriage. For a time George was more loving and attentive, but eventually he slipped back into his rigid posture. In the meantime, the delicate flirtation with Pattie by Eric Clapton continued, literally in front of George's eyes.

Once George and Eric returned from the Delaney and Bonnie tour, they resumed their friendship amid social gatherings at each other's homes. Eric now completely obsessed, was daring in his interactions with Pattie. They would make eyes at each other, hug and cuddle and whisper flirtatiously in each other's ears. Pattie did not take any of it seriously. George, likewise, would laugh it off, figuring that one of his best friends would not presume to make advances on his wife. What neither realized was that Eric was deadly serious in his pursuit of Pattie.

"What I couldn't accept was that she was out of reach for me," he would confess years later. "She was married to George and he was a mate but I had fallen in love and nothing else mattered."

Eric's obsession was increasing in its intensity. Although he could literally have any woman he wanted, he pursued and became romantically involved with Pattie's sister Paula, reasoning, he claimed, "that she looked a lot like Pattie and had the same kind of personality."

It came as no surprise that George was oblivious to what was going on. Flushed with a rush of creative energy after his return from the road, he had plunged headlong into a furious round of songwriting in preparation for his first solo album. While his religious beliefs colored much of his songwriting during this period, George's return to the rock life had infused him with a taste of rock-and-roll grit. George was excited at the possibilities.

In May 1970 George traveled to New York where he helped out Billy Preston on his latest album and spent a day with Bob Dylan in a Columbia Records recording studio, jamming. Little of what came out of that Dylan session has ever seen the light of day. But the vibe between the two musical giants was reportedly very good.

George returned to London and immediately began recording what would ultimately be a fifteen-song demo that included a wide array of songs stretching from his Beatles days to songs inspired by Dylan, to a couple of things, including the by-now completed "My Sweet Lord," that came from his time with the Delaney and Bonnie tour.

George settled on producer Phil Spector to guide *All Things Must Pass*, based primarily on the fact that he had made a silk purse out of the sow's ear of *Let It Be*. The musicians involved would be a Who's Who of stars and stellar session players including Eric Clapton, Ringo Starr, Klaus Voorman, Billy Preston, members of Badfinger, Jim Gordon, Bobby Whitlock, Gary Brooker, Bobby Keyes, and a then unknown sixteen-year-old named Phil Collins who was hired on for his ability on percussion.

Once the sessions began, the sheer volume of quality material began to beg the question of whether a single album would do justice to George's vision. Even George was unsure about what to do.

"When I started the album *All Things Must Pass* I was just trying to do a record and I had so many songs that we just recorded one after the other and just kept doing backing tracks. One day I thought, 'I better check out what's going on here,' and I had eighteen tracks. I thought, 'Well, I think that's probably enough,' and decided to put them all out at once."

While musically the sessions for *All Things Must Pass* were the classic meetings of good musicians and good vibes, the recording process was plagued by a number of fits and starts. Producer Phil Spector, known equally for his talents and eccentricities, allegedly took the occasion of *All Things Must Pass* to go on a protracted drinking binge. Plenty of brandy before going into the studio was not uncommon. Needless to say, George was not thrilled.

"I got so tired of that," he sadly recalled. "I needed someone to help. I was ending up with more work than if I'd just been doing it on my own."

Sadly, Louise Harrison's health began to fail around the time the *All Things Must Pass* sessions began, so George's thoughts were constantly on her. When she died in July 1970, the result of a brain hemorrhage, George was devastated and recording came to a halt for a number of weeks. There was talk that George would shut down the sessions permanently and the always present tabloids gossiped that George could not go on musically without his mother in his life and would never play or record again.

Adding further drama to the proceedings, Eric's pursuit of Pattie began to heat up.

Pattie began to realize that Eric's flirtation was serious when he phoned her one day and expressed his love for her. Pattie was astonished and insisted that such a relationship could not take place and that she loved George. However, Eric felt that Pattie had, in fact, been flattered.

Pattie would later reveal, "I couldn't believe the situation [Eric] had put me in. I thought it wasn't right and I thought it [our friendship] was destined to end."

But Eric persisted in his attempt to do the unthinkable . . . to steal the wife of a Beatle. One day an unsigned letter arrived at the Harrison home, addressed to Pattie. The letter, from Eric, said he needed to see her and that he loved her. Pattie, who has claimed she had no idea who the letter was from, immediately took it to George and explained that it was some crazy person who had written her. George did not take the letter or its implication seriously, and went about his business. The next night Eric called Pattie and confessed that he had written the letter. Pattie again protested that she was happily married. But in her private thoughts she could feel her resolve crumbling and her feelings for Eric increasing.

The sessions for *All Things Must Pass* resumed after George's period of mourning the death of his mother. What had initially been destined for a single album and then a double disc, was now evolving into a triple album, unheard-of at the time, thanks to an improvisational series of instrumental jams appropriately titled "Apple Jam." Eric, who at the time was doing some preliminary work on a solo project that would eventually evolve into Derek and the Dominos, was finding his musical interaction with George particularly intense— due, in varying degrees, to their mutual musical respect, his increased usage of drugs, and, in the back of his mind, the escalating pursuit of his best friend's wife.

"I'd set myself up to fail," he said years later, looking back on the situation. "It was an impossible situation. It was an impossible situation for Pattie to cope with or for me to cope with."

But it was an impossible situation that finally came to pass. *All Things Must Pass* had fallen behind schedule and George was spending more and more time in the final mixing stages to the exclusion of everything else in his life . . . including Pattie. On one particular night, George and Pattie had been invited to the London premiere of the avant-grade garde musical play *Oh, Calcutta!*

The situation was played out through two long-reported and divergent scenarios. Reportedly George was too busy working on the album to attend the premiere and did not blink an eye when Eric offered to escort Pattie. Another scenario had Eric showing up at the theater, spotting Pattie sitting alone at the other side of the theater and swapping seats with a stranger sitting next to her. The spark was finally lit at an after-theater party when Eric invited Pattie back to his house to hear some of the songs for the upcoming Derek and the Dominos record, including the song "Layla," allegedly inspired by Eric's unrequited love for Pattie. Pattie finally succumbed to Eric's subtle and sensitive nature and they made love for the first time.

George finally finished that evening's work and headed for the party to meet up with Pattie. As he drove up to the party, he spotted Eric and Pattie walking hand in hand, returning from their romantic rendezvous. George snapped, in an insanely jealous rage. He screamed at Eric, forbidding him to ever see his wife again, and shoved Pattie into his car and sped off.

The tension was thick for quite a few days after that. Amazingly, things soon returned to normal. It was as if George, either in denial or feeling extreme forgiveness for the betrayal, had put the incident completely out of his mind. Pattie was at her wit's end, her relationship with George and the intimacy she had shared with Eric a jumble of conflicting emotions. In a way, the incident made her love George all the more. But for the better part of a year, she would continue to sneak off to be with Eric.

A number of theories have been advanced over the years in an attempt to explain George's reaction. His religion had guided him to a highly evolved spiritual place. He so valued his friendship with Eric that he was turning a blind eye to the affair. There was also the fact that his eye was beginning to wander as well.

Groupies, dubbed "scruffs" by the musicians, had taken to hanging outside the studio where *All Things Must Pass* was being recorded, with much of their attention being channeled toward George. In return, George was generous to the attentions of his fans, signing autographs, posing for pictures, and chatting them up. Carol Bedford, who had come all the way from Texas to be a scruff, was a different story.

Her beauty, spirit, and youth had struck an unexpected emotional chord in George. Although keeping things on a strictly platonic level in and around the studio, Carol was sparking a barely-below-the-surface streak of romantic/lustful interest. George's loyalty to his by-now unfaithful wife slipped one night when he showed up unexpectedly at Carol Bedford's flat. They hugged and chatted for a few moments. Carol recalled that George was nervous and frightened as they made their way to her bedroom. Carol vividly remembered what happened next.

"He looked shy. He stepped towards me and placed his arms around me. I thought he just wanted to hug me as he had when he arrived. But he kissed me. Needless to say, I happily responded."

It went no further but, for the next two years, George and Carol would stay in touch on a friendship basis. Carol sensed that George wanted to take the relationship further and that he was struggling with his conscience about whether or not to betray his vows.

The music industry held its breath as *All Things Must Pass* made its December bow. Double albums were considered an act of self-indulgence under the best of circumstances. A triple album, even by no less a personage than George Harrison, was considered commercial suicide. For his part, George was quietly confident that he had done the right thing. Ever the realist and the cynic, John Lennon was one of the most vocal naysayers of George's album.

"I remember John was really negative at the time," said George. "John saw the album cover and said, 'He must be fucking mad, putting three records out.' There was a lot of negativity going down. I just felt that whatever happened, whether it was a flop or a success, I was gonna go on my own just to have a bit of peace of mind."

All Things Must Pass was an immediate worldwide hit, moving almost immediately to number one on both the British and U.S. charts. "My Sweet Lord," George's first attempt at gospel, became the first single off the album and would go on to sell more than five million copies worldwide.

George's joy at the success of *All Things Must Pass* was short-lived. In March 1971, the music-publishing company Bright Tunes, which owned the copyright on the Chiffons song "He's So Fine," filed a plagiarism suit against George Harrison, charging that the former Beatle had borrowed too liberally from that song in the creation of "My Sweet Lord." George steadfastly denied the claim, saying that any inspiration for the song actually came from the Edwin Hawkins Singers hit "Oh Happy Day." But there were many who offered that, figuratively and literally, George had been caught with his hand in the cookie jar.

"He walked right into it," recalled John Lennon. "He knew what he was doing. He must have known. He's smarter than that. He could have changed a couple of bars in that song and nobody could ever have touched him. But he just let it go and paid the price. Maybe he thought God would just sort of let him off."

Delaney Bramlett, who essentially laid out the blueprint for the song during the Delaney and Bonnie and Friends tour, was equally surprised and somewhat perturbed when he heard "My Sweet Lord" coming out of every radio in the land.

"I called up George and told him that I didn't mean for him to use the melody of 'He's So Fine.' He said, 'Well, it's not exactly,' and it really wasn't. He did put some curves in there but he did get sued."

Delaney became even more upset when he went out and bought the record and discovered that only George was credited with writing the song. "When I saw I wasn't credited, I called George and said, 'George, I didn't see my name on the song.' He promised me that it would be on the next printing of the record. I was never given credit on that song but he did admit that the song, to a large extent, was mine, and I never saw any money from it."

Delaney was upset but refused to pursue his legitimate complaint in the courts. His feeling was that he would not give up his friendship with George for a song. Unfortunately, George did not feel the same way.

"We haven't spoken since all that came about. It makes me feel sad. There are no hard feelings from me. I believe, because we haven't spoken in years, that he felt worse about it than I did. I just think the whole thing was an oversight on his part. He just didn't follow through on it."

The lawsuit would eventually wend its way through the court system and go to trial in 1976. George did not delve on it for long and, as always, let his lawyers hash out his legal problems while he moved on to more enjoyable pursuits. Under the pseudonym of George O'Hara Smith, George helped out on albums by friends and acquaintances—playing guitar on albums by Ashton, Gardner and Dyke; Gary Wright; and Billy Preston. Under his own name, he produced an album for Ravi Shankar and, showing there were no hard feelings about Lennon's *All Things Must Pass* slam, George played guitar and dobro on John's solo album *Imagine*.

With all the competitive angst behind them, the relationship between George and John had improved dramatically.

George, now well into what was being considered a success-ful solo career, had grown in confidence in his dealings with John, and, by association, John, who had long respected George as a guitarist, had grasped on to his maturity as an all-around performer and a person. Thus it had been a happy occasion, beginning in 1969 with the Instant Karma and Plastic Ono Band, when John would willingly embrace George's skills and invite him to play in his solo world. For his part, George could not have been more happy. And while he was thrilled when John asked him to come over and help out on what would become his landmark album, *Imagine*, George would recall that some of the old tensions were simmering beneath the surface during the sessions.

"It was nerve-wracking, as usual. At that time, very strange, intense feelings were going on. I knew Klaus Voorman was working with John and so I called over one day to find out what was going on. John said, 'Oh, you know, you should come over.' So I just put my guitar and amplifier in the car and went over. I turned up and he was openly pleased that I came."

At home, George and Pattie personal life continued to unravel in an almost surreal way. By this time George was well aware that Pattie and Eric were having an affair. But rather than macho posturing and physical violence, neither of which would have been in keeping with George's character, he went on as if nothing was wrong and, in fact, seemed to bend over backward to encourage his wife and his best friend.

"Actually, Pattie and I had been splitting up for years," he candidly explained. "That was the funny thing, you know. I thought that was the best thing to do, for us to split, and we should have just done it much sooner. But I didn't have any problem about it. Eric had the problem. Every time I'd go and see him, he'd be really hung up about it, and I was saying,

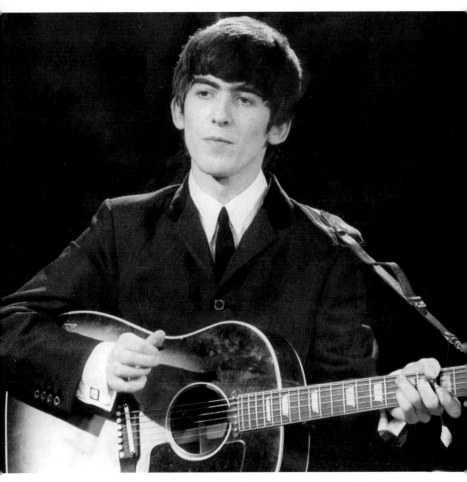

Harrison performing in concert with the Beatles, December 3, 1963.
HULTON/ARCHIVE BY GETTY IMAGES

Previous page: Taking a break from playing at the Cavern in Liverpool,
c. 1960.
HULTON/ARCHIVE BY GETTY IMAGES

The Beatles with Ed Sullivan at the NBC studios, New York City,
February 9, 1964. (*Left to right*): Ringo Starr, George Harrison,
Ed Sullivan, John Lennon, and Paul McCartney.
BERNARD GOTFRYD/HULTON/ARCHIVE BY GETTY IMAGES

John Lennon, George Harrison, Paul McCartney, and Ringo Starr,
pictured on their arrival in London following a tour of Australia,
July 2, 1964.
HULTON/ARCHIVE BY GETTY IMAGES

George Harrison and his
bride, twenty-one-year-
old model Pattie Boyd,
leaving Epsom Registry
Office in London, after
their marriage,
January 24, 1966.
HULTON/ARCHIVE BY
GETTY IMAGES

Harrison with his wife, Pattie Boyd, on their honeymoon in
Barbados, February 14, 1966.
HULTON/ARCHIVE BY GETTY IMAGES

Harrison with his wife, Pattie Boyd, as they leave Esher and Walton Magistrates Court, following a £250 fine for possession of cannabis, March 31, 1969.

Bob Dylan performs with Harrison at the Concert for Bangladesh at
Madison Square Garden, New York City, August 8, 1971.
HULTON/ARCHIVE BY GETTY IMAGES

Left: Harrison at a concert in Copenhagen with Eric Clapton and Delaney
and Bonnie, December 13, 1969.
HULTON/ARCHIVE BY GETTY IMAGES

Harrison with Indian sitar maestro Ravi Shankar, during the time Harrison helped to organize the Concert
for Bangladesh, December 1971.

George Harrison
poses with his
wife, Olivia.

'Fuck it, man. Don't be apologizing,' and he didn't believe me. I was saying, 'I don't care.' "

While George seemed to take the high road, there was much in his actions that, perhaps deliberately, was destined to cause his wife and his best friend the maximum amount of pain and discomfort—revenge, if you will—in a way that only a quiet man like George Harrison could inflict it. And the reality was that Pattie and Eric's love affair had, indeed, spiraled down into a pool of guilt and frustration.

"I felt terrible guilt," remembered Pattie. "Eric kept insisting I should leave George and go and live with him. I said I couldn't. I got cold feet. I couldn't bear it."

Eric's guilt at betraying his best friend was instrumental in his descent into hard-drug use and, in particular, heroin. And although he professed to love Pattie with all his heart, he would use his addiction as the ultimate threat the night Pattie told Eric she could not see him anymore.

"I told her that either she came with me or I hit the deck," Eric reflected painfully. "I actually presented her with a packet of heroin and said, 'If you don't come with me, I'm taking this for the next couple of years.' I put dreadful, dreadful pressure on her, but I couldn't help myself. I really could not visualize a life without her. Well, the pressure from me must have been so great that she went back and closed herself back into the house and George."

George Harrison had, whether intentionally or not, lost his wife and driven his best friend to heroin addiction. George Harrison had won.

nine

All Things Must Pass

As with all wars, it was the innocents who paid the heavy price.

In 1971, the war between West and East Pakistan was fought over freedom; the desire of East Pakistanis (whose province would later come to be known as Bangladesh) to be free resulted in a bitter battle that sent hundreds of thousands of East Pakistani refugees fleeing across the border to nearby Calcutta where a lack of food and sanitary conditions was resulting in the death of thousands on a daily basis. And, as always, those who suffered the most were the children.

Ravi Shankar, who had many distant relatives among the refugees, was particularly concerned and sensitive to the suffering, especially the suffering of the children. "The idea occurred to me of giving a concert to raise money to help these refugees, something on a bigger-than-normal scale. At the time, George Harrison was in Los Angeles and had come to visit me. I asked him frankly, 'George, can you help me?' Because I knew that if I gave a concert myself, I would not be able to raise a significant amount. George was really moved and said, 'Yes, something should be done.' That was when he wrote the song 'Bangla Desh.' "

But George had more on his mind than a simple song extolling the plight of the refugees. "I said, 'Okay, I'll go on the show and I'll get some other people to come and help. We'll try and make it into a big show and maybe we can make a million dollars instead of a few thousand.' So I got on the telephone trying to round people up."

That George agreed so readily to become involved should not have come as a surprise. His life was marked by small moments of generous acts. He had always maintained a soft spot in his heart for the downtrodden, more so since he had come to embrace Hinduism. He had always been quick with a check or a handful of bills. But he saw in responding to Shankar's request the opportunity to use the talent that God had given him to truly help out those in need on a massive scale. The plight of Bangladesh truly touched his heart and soul.

But George had an ulterior motive for trying to put together an all-star lineup of performers. The reality was that George was terrified of the responsibility of having to head-line a show that size. Of course he wanted a massive roster of artists to help put the charity concerts over the top. Perhaps he was scared at the prospect of standing in the spotlight alone.

George was wildly successful at getting other respected musicians to climb aboard. He managed to talk Bob Dylan, who had been reclusive for a number of years, into partici-pating. Given the real and imagined tensions between them, it was surprising that Eric Clapton, by now in the midst of a full-blown heroin addiction, also agreed to play. Billy Preston, Leon Russell, Jesse Ed Davis, Klaus Voorman, and Ringo Starr were also willing to lend their time and talent.

For a time in the preparation for the Concerts for Bangladesh, there was a rumor circulating that this might be the first live appearance of the Beatles since 1966. John had initially jumped at the chance to perform but backed out when George insisted that Yoko could not perform. As for Paul, he had expressed some interest early on but, perhaps still smarting from the ongoing legal entanglements centered around the end of the Beatles, finally said no.

George was particularly disappointed at John's refusal to play at Bangladesh, and in fact felt John owed George his participation because of all the help George felt he had given John over the years. In actuality, John's refusal to honor George's request went further than George's refusing to allow Yoko to perform. John was notorious for detesting doing charity benefits and was not about to change his attitude, even for George. But truth be known, there was also a bit of jealousy of George on John's part. Because at the same time George's *All Things Must Pass* was released to rave reviews and massive sales, John's largely experimental album *Primal Screams* was also released to only marginal reviews and poor sales. John took it personally and as a real assault by George on his still-perceived leadership in the Beatles universe. George took John's "no" at his word and moved on.

"We pinpointed the days that were astrologically good," recalled George of his plans for the charity event, "and we found Madison Square Garden was open on one of those days."

George ever the consummate businessman, began looking for ways to maximize this charitable good work. He engaged the services of Phil Spector to record the concert for an album to be released later. He also arranged for a concert film to be made. When, following a July 27 press conference in which George and Ravi Shankar made an impassioned and enlightened plea for help, the first show quickly sold out, George arranged for a second show to be held on August 1. George Harrison was at his philanthropic best with the Concerts for Bangladesh.

Unfortunately, the occasion of the Concerts for Bangladesh would also expose his weakness as a human being.

For years there were rumors that George had, in fact, been involved in numerous adulterous affairs and that he considered Pattie's affair with Eric tacit permission for him to do the same. But none had ever been confirmed and George would often acknowledge that he had remained faithful to Pattie.

Two days before the concert, George Harrison succumbed to temptation.

During the last-minute, pre-concert preparations, George was being hustled through a hotel lobby when he came across a bright-eyed, attractive twenty-year-old woman who, in later years, would be known only as Maralyn. George looked into the young woman's eyes and there was an instant connection. George stopped dead in his tracks and chatted with Maralyn. As he was finally hustled away by his entourage, he reportedly told Maralyn, "Why don't you hang out and maybe I'll see you later on?"

Maralyn was happily shocked by this encounter and did continue to hang out in the hotel lobby. Maralyn, in later accounts of the incident, explained how, a few hours later, one of George's assistants returned to the lobby and escorted her to George's room. She recalled George appeared uncomfortable with the situation as the pair engaged in uneasy small talk alone. Finally George made his move and the pair were soon making love on his bed. Maralyn recalled George being a strong, considerate lover, and after a prolonged period of intimacy, they showered, took a nap, and George taught Maralyn how to chant.

George would continue to see Maralyn for a period of time after that encounter, and it was during those occasions that he opened up to the woman. She related that George was in a really bad period in his life and that, although George and Pattie made a point of arriving and leaving social functions together, their marriage had by that time dissolved into something closer to a brother-sister relationship in which they were both free to do what they liked.

But while his personal life was a mess, George managed to pull together a truly fantastic musical experience with the Concerts for Bangladesh. The musicians performed a wide variety of songs in an electric atmosphere that went well beyond a mere charity concert; becoming a legitimate musical event easily rivaling, according to some reviews, the best moments of Woodstock. When the dust settled, a total of fifteen million dollars had been raised to aid the Bangladesh refugees. But George's pride in his good work would be tarnished almost immediately.

He was soon informed that both American and British tax officials were poised to take their cuts of the proceeds. George met with the tax people and was passionate in telling the administrators that the money was going to help humanity and to save lives. The tax people were not interested and, in the end, George wrote a personal check in the amount of one million pounds to cover the taxes.

George and Phil Spector did a yeoman's job in mixing the concert and, on December 20, 1971, a mammoth three-record live set, *The Concert for Bangladesh*, was released. In order to bring in as much money as possible for the cause, George insisted that the three-record set be reasonably priced, at nine dollars. Unfortunately, George could not prevent unscrupulous record-store owners from jacking up the price to eighteen dollars and pocketing the extra money for themselves.

For George, much of the goodwill and spirit of giving that he had put into helping the Bangladesh refugees was now lost. But he would be buoyed by reports that the concerts and records not only succeeded in collecting millions of dollars for the refugees but, of equal importance, raised the world's awareness of the plight of the people of Bangladesh.

George, flushed with the success of *All Things Must Pass* and boosted spiritually by the success of his good works with the Concerts for Bangladesh, was now making plans to return to the recording studio to record his second solo album, *Living in the Material World*. During this period, George's sense of religious fervor was at an all-time high and he insisted that his new album would have as its primary goal getting the word of Krishna and God out to the masses.

That George was continuing his very un-Krishna ways of drinking, drug-taking, and womanizing seemed to be lost on the musician, who, typically, seemed to ignore the fact that he might be acting the hypocrite in the public eye. Apparently, a combination of ego, conviction, and a surprising sense of immaturity when it came to his vices, seemed to convince George that he did not have a problem.

True to his promise, *Living in the Material World* was populated by thinly disguised polemics about the love of Krishna that were nothing if not maudlin and self-indulgent. In fact, only "Sue Me Sue You Blues" showed any real sense of bite and real-world irony.

George should have known better than to ask Phil Spector to once again produce *Living in the Material World*. But he did anyway, and so he was destined to have the same problems that he had had on *All Things Must Pass*. Spector was constantly drunk and unavailable. George was spending more and more time trying to rouse the eccentric producer and getting him to the studio. Finally he just gave up and, for all intents and purposes, ended up producing the album himself.

Like his previous album, making music was George's salvation and, with the aid of musical friends that included Ringo, Nicky Hopkins, Gary Wright, and Klaus Voorman, the sessions for *Living in the Material World* ran smoothly, as George extolled the virtues of Krishna in such songs as "The Lord Loves the One Who Loves the Lord" and "The Light that Has Lighted the World." Once again the music industry predicted a dire fate for George's latest effort. And once again George was confident his music and—by association—his beliefs would be upheld in the court of public opinion and commerce.

Living in the Material World was released in May 1973. George again had the last laugh as the album, despite its many detractors, crashed the top of the charts in England and the United States. The first single, "Give Me Love (Give Me Peace on Earth)," which encapsulated George's religious attitude in a light-pop framework, also went to number one.

In the wake of the success of his latest album, George was encouraged to tour for the first time as a solo artist. He was tempted but ultimately passed on the opportunity, preferring to return to his reclusive nature, his unhappy marriage, a religious worldview that bounced back and forth between strident fervor, and a drugs-and-sex heathenism that flew in the face of that selfsame belief. That George was confused at this point in his life was a given; anger and impatience were emotions that his close circle of friends had come to expect.

"He has his black moods, and God help anyone who at

that time incites his wrath," close friend Ravi Shankar once said. "He can be very hard. He doesn't hide his feelings. He can also completely shut himself off and be quite indifferent and distrustful. Of course, this is understandable, because he has been so exploited by people he has trusted. It is a wonder he is not like that all the time."

It was in this time of turmoil that George Harrison turned thirty.

Needless to say, George's dark mood during this period only added to the emotional pain Pattie was suffering. Desperate to escape the restrictive boundaries set up by George, she began doing charity work, attempting to master the piano and violin, and would often consult psychics in an effort to discover what she should do with her life.

"I just don't want to be the little wife sitting at home," she explained at the time. "I want to do something worthwhile."

George's downward spiral continued. His drug use increased and he gave up all pretense of fidelity, actively and sexually attempting to seduce every woman he met. And it did not make any difference if the woman was available or not. In a scenario very reminiscent of the situation between Pattie and Eric, George had reestablished a strong relationship with Ringo and his wife Maureen. The two couples would get together socially at each other's homes, and it soon became apparent, at least to Pattie, that her husband had more than a friendly interest in Maureen.

One night Ringo and Maureen invited George and Pattie to their home for dinner. After dinner, and in a mellow mood, George picked up a guitar and began playing some love songs. Suddenly he stopped playing, looked at Maureen who was sitting next to Ringo and said, "I'm in love with you, Maureen." Maureen was visibly upset. Ringo raged at George and then stormed out of the room. Pattie, totally mortified at this latest embarrassment, burst into tears and locked herself in Ringo's bathroom.

The evening was ruined. But once she got over the shock, Maureen was flattered by George's bravado and—as her marriage with Ringo was also going through a rough patch—more than a little bit interested. A few weeks later, Pattie returned from shopping and found George and Maureen in bed together. For Pattie, this was the last straw. George did not think twice about the incident, and in fact would continue his affair with Maureen for a period of time, eventually being named as the major cause of the breakup of Ringo and Maureen's marriage a couple of years later. When he was asked by an acquaintance how he could have an affair with the wife of one of his best friends, George reportedly shrugged his shoulders and said, "Incest, I guess."

With the situation all but hopeless, George's bravado unavoidably sank into a period of despair midway through 1973. In a candid conversation with his good friend musician Gary Wright, he spilled his guts about his state of mind regarding his relationship with Pattie when he said, "I really do love Pattie. But it's almost as though love alone isn't enough."

George returned home from his conversation with Wright determined to try and patch up his relationship with Pattie. Unfortunately, he found that Pattie was no longer the loving, submissive woman he had loved and so often betrayed. Pattie was now openly defiant and, for the first time in years, totally independent. She ignored his wishes and, although they continued to live under the same roof, they rarely spoke.

Pattie resumed her modeling career and, happily, discovered she was still much in demand. Also, most likely in response to George's recent philandering, she openly flaunted a brief affair with former Small Faces and future Rolling Stone guitarist Ron Wood.

George was reportedly beside himself with guilt and sadness, and was feeling himself slipping out of control of his life. Early in 1974, George did what he always seemed to do when pushed into a corner, he turned inward and toward his religion. More specifically, he traveled to India where he spent several weeks wandering happily among holy shrines, meeting with several spiritual advisors, and praying. He felt enlightened and encouraged by this spiritual odyssey and was sure he could now return to England and, somehow, pull together his life with Pattie.

What he did not know was that Pattie was on an odyssey of her own.

She flew to Los Angeles to spend time with her sister Jenny, who was married to Fleetwood Mac drummer Mick Fleetwood. Pattie, who stayed at the Beverly Hills Hotel during her stay in Los Angeles, also spent some time with Delaney and Bonnie Bramlett in their southern California home. Pattie spent a few days with the Bramletts, catching up on old times. Delaney sensed from those conversations that Pattie and George's marriage was in trouble, but it was not his nature to pry.

One day Pattie asked Delaney if he would drive her back to her hotel so she could get a change of clothes. They drove to the hotel. It was at the hotel that Delaney received the surprise of his life.

"She said she was only going to change clothes, but all of a sudden she started coming on to me in an aggressive, romantic way. She was just very friendly, let me put it to you that way."

Delaney admitted he was having trouble in his own marriage at the time, and that, under different circumstances, something most likely would have happened.

"If it hadn't been for my friendship with George, something would have happened," said Delaney "But I wasn't about to do anything that would harm our friendship. I think she gathered that when I would bring up George's name every two or three seconds and made up some excuse about having to get back to the studio. I think she was a little upset that I was not responding to her. I think she thought I didn't think she was attractive or something."

Pattie eventually backed off and they returned to Delaney's house. Nothing more was said about the incident but, for a long time afterward, Delaney feared that the reason he had not heard from George was that Pattie had said something to George about what happened.

"I was afraid that Pattie might have gotten mad and said, 'Well, Delaney and I did this and such.' If that had happened, it would have killed me. It would have broken my heart."

Delaney assumed that Pattie flew back to London after her Los Angeles visit. The reality was that she had flown to Miami where Eric Clapton was working on his latest album, *461 Ocean Boulevard*. They laid their cards on the table. Pattie admitted that she had been manipulating Eric in an attempt to recapture George's love but that she was over that now and was truly in love with Eric. They both realized it had been their respective loneliness and neediness that had drawn them together and that the love they had been feeling for each other was real.

Upon his return from India, Pattie informed George that

she was again with Eric and that she was not coming back. George was sad but philosophical as he reflected on his loss. "It's no big deal. We've separated many times but this time I don't know what will happen. In this life, there is no time to lose in an uncomfortable situation."

With this revelation, George took on a sincere strength regarding the relationship. His tacit approval of the infidelity continued to play on Eric's mind. And it forced Eric's hand. He knew that Pattie at that point was essentially his, but his friendship with George necessitated that he confront George. And so at a party not too long after completing *461 Ocean Boulevard*, Eric, with Pattie present, confronted George.

"I went straight up to him and said, 'I'm in love with your wife. What are you going to do about it?' George said, 'Whatever you like, man. It doesn't worry me.' He was being very spiritual about it and saying everybody should do their own thing. He then said, 'You can have her and I'll have your girlfriend.' I couldn't believe this. I thought he was going to chin me. Pattie freaked out and ran away. Suddenly she was in limbo. George must have been very upset too. But that's crazy! If he didn't want her to leave him, he shouldn't have let me take her."

But while he was putting up a brave front, George did not take the unofficial end of his marriage well. As with other stressful moments in his life, George turned to the bottle to salve his pain and, according to his close friends, was reportedly flirting with full-blown alcoholism. While he would often deny during that period that he was a alcoholic, George would concede that he was putting away quite a bit of drink as well as an extreme amount of psychedelics.

George continued to indulge in largely meaningless affairs— the most significant being with model Kathy Simmonds with whom he lived for a time in a villa on the island of Grenada. George could very easily take some time off and rest on his laurels. But he was morose and maudlin and appeared a walking example of clinical depression. Pure and simple, George Harrison was not happy. Which was why in this time of emotional crisis, he turned to the one thing he could count on to make him happy: his music.

George's ego knew no bounds thanks to the back-to-back successes of *All Things Must Pass* and *Living in the Material World*. He was also quick to remind people that, after playing second fiddle to Lennon and McCartney for lo these many years, he had been the most commercially successful ex-Beatle in the undeclared race of solo projects. It was also in this state of egomania that George committed extreme blasphemy.

He said the Beatles had been shit.

"Having played with other musicians, I don't even think the Beatles were that good," he once said in an interview. "It's all a fantasy, this idea of putting the Beatles back together again. The only way it will happen is if we're all broke. Even then, I wouldn't relish playing with Paul. He's a fine bass player but he's sometimes overpowering. Ringo's got the best backbeat in the business and I'd join a band with John Lennon any day. But I wouldn't join a band with Paul McCartney. That's not personal; it's from a musician's point of view. The biggest break in my career was getting in the Beatles. The second-biggest break since then was getting out of them."

Needless to say, George's remarks eventually made their way back to John, Paul, and Ringo. While specific responses were not forthcoming, it was safe to say that George's comments had, especially in the case of Paul, aggravated an already antagonistic relationship between the four ex-mates that, in ensuing years, often found them sniping at each other in interviews.

For better or worse, a combination of George's ego and his commercial success had succeeded in bringing down a long-held wall. George was finally ready to tour as a solo act.

"He was definitely inspired [to tour] after Bangladesh," remembered George's close friend Billy Preston. "He wanted to do it again right away. But it took some time. He had to do a lot of thinking on this one because he had to get out there and be the one."

Many point to George's sudden confidence in returning to touring to his friendship with Ravi Shankar and his love for Indian music. Shankar himself felt that what George had been hearing in India had ultimately turned George in the direction of touring.

"George heard a few tapes I had of things with groups and he was impressed and was telling me that I should bring something like this over [to the States]. Well, I said, 'You must also take part in it.' "

However, George's creative side had company; a sense that he needed to stretch as a businessman. Which meant addressing the issue of Apple Records.

"Apple was just going through such chaos from a business point of view and at the time John and Paul didn't really wanna know. They were getting ready to sweep Apple Records underneath the carpet. Ringo and I were planning to try and keep it going and there was so many problems just from old contracts that, for me, it seemed simpler just to start afresh."

Hence the inspiration for Dark Horse Records, in which George would oversee a small roster of eclectic artists, chosen by, and for the most part produced by, George. Ideally, it would be a label that would release all of George's solo LPs but, unfortunately, he was still tied to Apple until 1976. But that did not deter A&M Records from negotiating a deal with Harrison to distribute the label in May 1974.

Flush with his Dark Horse deal and feeling totally invincible in the face of the seeming tower of responsibility over him, George relocated to Los Angeles and began sifting through the mound of demo tapes by artists hoping to land a deal with Dark Horse.

In short order, George had selected the pop duo Splinter and old friend Ravi Shankar to be Dark Horse's first artists. For the Splinter album, George enlisted Klaus Voorman and the usual group of seasoned session players to add substance to what could have been a thin pop effort. For the Ravi Shankar album, he employed an improvisational approach in which Shankar and a group of musicians that included Ringo, Klaus Voorman, and Billy Preston created the music in the studio. Shankar recalled that, despite the obvious stress in George's life, his friend was fairly laid-back and relaxed during the recording, and he brought what Shankar considered a heightened sense of spirituality to the proceedings.

Earlier in the year, George had visited his old friend Ravi Shankar in India and, inspired by the possibilities of spreading both religion and Krishna consciousness, had urged Ravi to join his tour as an opening act. And Ravi related that George's plans were expansive. A Boeing 707, complete with the religious symbol the Aum painted on the outside of the plane, would be outfitted inside in pure Indian opulence. Indian food would be provided at every stop of the tour.

Throughout late summer and into fall, George was a one-person dynamo of activity. He had begun work on the album *Dark Horse* while at the same time he was hiring respected musicians including Tom Scott, Robben Ford, old friend Billy Preston, Andy Newmark, and Willie Weeks, and beginning rehearsals for the tour which was set to begin in November. At the same time, George was also taking care of the Dark Horse Records business.

When it came to the latter situation, he was being aided greatly by an industrious and conscientious secretary that A&M Records had hired for him named Olivia Trinidad Arias. The twenty seven-year-old Mexican-born Arias was, for George, the one stable element in his otherwise chaotic world. When calling about business, George could count on Olivia having everything under control. George was impressed by her business acumen and, reading between the lines, her calm, unflappable nature. George would look forward to his calls to the office and often called up for no other reason than to chat. No matter what was going on during the course of his day, George would often find himself thinking about Olivia . . . and—without having met her face-to-face—falling in love with her.

But George knew he had to be careful. Over the course of numerous relationships over a lifetime, he had become leery of women who wanted to be involved with him for material gain or as a career springboard. And so, with his cynicism never too far from the surface, George contacted some associates in California and not-too-delicately asked that Olivia be checked out. When it was discovered that Olivia had no secrets or hidden agendas, George was thrilled. George visited

Dark Horse Records for the first time in 1974 and there met
Olivia for the first time.

It was love at first sight.

Behind the dark-haired, clear-eyed beauty was a spiritual
and soulful side that was very much in sync with George's
personality. Olivia was a strong woman, fully capable of handling life, and sensitive to the needs of George who seemed
to still need a bit of mothering to take the edge off. Olivia
was also practical and wise in the way of the real world and
would prove a credible sounding-board for George's often
reckless and naive approach to the business side of life. In
George, Olivia saw a strong-willed yet sensitive man who had
love in his heart and would be the ideal companion. In no
time at all George and Olivia had formed what, for George,
would be a true love match.

Which, by October 1974, was exactly what George
needed. He was burning the candle at too many ends.
George had hoped to complete *Dark Horse* at a leisurely pace
and still have time to rest before beginning his thirty-day
North American "George Harrison and Friends" tour in
November. But his meticulous nature in the studio had
resulted in the *Dark Horse* sessions falling behind. On top of
that, George's normally mellifluous singing voice was being
ground down by the hellish recording and rehearsal schedule
to the point where it was now little more than a hoarse
croak.

George would later admit that he was "physically run-
down" and by the time the tour started he was, more often
than not, "tired and wiped out."

But George's physical well-being was not the only concern
in the days leading up to the tour's start in Vancouver.
George's insistence that the Ravi Shankar Orchestra perform

an extra-long opening set had promoter Bill Graham and even George's most devoted business partners concerned about the potential for dampening what had been built up in the press as a "George Harrison rock concert." George's reluctance to do only a handful of the more commercially oriented Beatles and George Harrison songs and the vast majority of lower-profile religiously oriented songs, also had people crossing their fingers. Would George's insistence on turning his first solo tour into a grand-scale revival meeting hit, or miss?

The postmortem following that first show cut like a knife. And most of the cuts quite justifiably drew blood. The crowd—once the initial excitement of being at a former Beatle's concert had worn off—had been largely unresponsive and bored during Ravi Shankar's set; a situation made all the more aggravating by the fact that George had allowed Ravi's orchestra to do an extended interlude in his nearly two-and-a-half-hour set. George's weak, off-key voice was death even to the set's more introspective songs and, unfortunately, there were a lot of those. Throughout the show, George chose to ignore the audience's impatient crys of "Get funky!" and "Rock and roll!" When the audience response was not to his liking, he would admonish them for sitting on their hands. When he felt like it, George would change the lyrics to many of his songs to reflect his Krishna consciousness and his between-song patter seemed more inclined to winning religious converts than a legitimate audience exchange.

Consequently, while the press found much to attack in the next day's reviews, the worst critiques came from those within George's inner circle.

"I hated it," said Pat Luce, a Dark Horse publicist who was in attendance at the Vancouver show. "In the framework of the show, there is a fabulous show. But one, it's too long; two, Ravi's got to be one set. And three, George has got to shut up."

George steadfastly refused to knuckle under, insisting his way was the right way. But when audiences continued to be underwhelmed and bored by shows in Seattle and San Francisco and reviewers continued to slam George's performance, promoter Bill Graham, never one to pull punches, got into the act. He met with Tom Scott and George's business manager, Denis O'Brien, presenting them with pages of suggestions on what he felt George had to do to improve the quality of the show. However, it was Graham's respect for George's artistic quality and talents that kept him from approaching George himself.

"With George Harrison, the audience would definitely have wanted more of George Harrison," Graham said, choosing his words carefully. "[The audience] perhaps had a feeling of bittersweetness about not having gotten just a bit closer to what their expectations were. They didn't get to go back in the time machine enough."

But George refused to budge from his notion of rock-and-roll show as religious revival. And so George continued to preach from his pulpit and the crowds continued to grow angry at their idol's pompousness. It made for some ugly moments during the early stages of the tour.

During one show, George stopped in midset and urged the crowd, "I want you all to chant 'Hare Hare!' " When the audience response was not to his liking, George became miffed and yelled at the crowd, "I don't know what you think, but from up here you sound pretty dead."

At another disastrous low point in the tour, George, his voice barely above a whisper, ranted at an obviously bored and lethargic audience. "I'd just like to tell you that the Lord is in your hearts. I'm not up here jumping like a loony for my own sake but to tell you that the Lord is in your hearts. Somebody's got to tell you. Let us reflect him in one another." There was a scattering of boos and catcalls as well as frustrated requests for Beatles songs. People began leaving in droves as George continued to rave.

After the first disastrous shows, Tom Scott, Billy Preston, Ravi Shankar, and others met with George and delicately suggested some changes. Shankar was quietly adamant that perhaps he should be limited to just an opening set. While George grudgingly agreed to shorten Shankar's participation, he steadfastly refused to alter his show in any other way and, as the tour continued, he became increasingly impatient and angry with his audience. He would scold them when they would not respond to Shankar's set or his own Krishna-based songs. As if to further frustrate audiences, he took to altering lyrics to the Beatles songs as well as some of his better-known solo material.

George remained defiant as the poor response and savage reviews continued to dog the tour. "You know, I didn't force you or anybody at gunpoint to come and see me," said Harrison backstage before one of the concerts. "And I don't care if nobody comes to see me. I don't give a shit. It doesn't matter to me. I'm going to do what I feel within myself."

Unfortunately, this was not an isolated outburst. With the negative vibe a constant companion on the tour, George was at his most moody, altering, sometimes on an hourly basis, between cynicism and euphoria. There were charges, made primarily through George's business manager, that Ravi Shankar had been taking advantage of him financially—a charge George would vehemently deny.

By the time the George Harrison and Friends tour concluded with a Madison Square Garden show in New York on December 20, 1974, George was fairly happy with the results. The tour, despite often playing to less-than-full houses, had managed to gross a quite respectable four million dollars. While never spectacular, through a gradually lessening of expectations by reviewers and audiences alike, the concerts had evolved into a good, if never great, experience. George was happy with small victories.

But one need only look into his eyes and assay his body language to know that the tour had ended just in time. And that the best Christmas present anybody could give him would be to leave him alone . . .

And let him rest.

In the days and weeks following the conclusion of the tour, George would publicly speculate that his first solo tour would most likely be his last. The less-than-stellar response to the tour was said to be a contributing factor. The physical and emotional rigors of touring also could be considered a defining moment in his decision not to tour again. But George, in looking back on the 1974 tour, felt there was a philosophical reason never to perform again.

"I'd go out there onstage and you'd just get stoned because there was so much reefer going about. I just thought, 'Do I actually have anything in common with these people?' "

ten
In Sickness and in Health

Dark Horse was a true reflection of George Harrison's dark mood.

Far less religious in tone than his previous solo albums, *Dark Horse* was nevertheless a low-key musical barometer of how far George's mental outlook had disintegrated. Always big on irony, George recruited Pattie to sing backup vocals on his cover of the Everly Brothers' classic "Bye Bye Love." The first single off the album, "Ding Dong" had as its B-side the non-album cut "I Don't Care Anymore." *Dark Horse* was, in essence, George Harrison throwing in the towel, throwing up his hands and surrendering.

This was a difficult album for audiences. The solemn nature turned off those who had become accustomed to George's sense of spiritual hope and, as had been the case with previous albums, the dearth of pure pop and rock canceled out those who continued to hope against hope for a truly Beatles-type album from George. Consequently, *Dark Horse*, while the single struggled to crack the Top 40 in the U.S. and England, the album topped out at number 36 in the States while it failed to chart in the U.K.

Following his 1974 tour, George and Olivia retreated to his England home. Press interest in George remained high and it was with increasing reluctance that he continued to do interviews, most focusing on the critical failure of both the tour and the *Dark Horse* album. While he stated that neither bothered him, his words rang false. To the world at large, George was either fooling himself or denying the obvious, which was that in the one area he could always count on for solace, he was now vulnerable.

Away from the public eye, George was now in a personal hell of his own making. His musical failures had dragged him into a deep depression and, while he was loath to admit it, the consensus was that Pattie's leaving him had also cut deep. The change in George became evident throughout 1975. He could be wildly social when he wanted to be, but George now rarely left his home and had cut himself off from all his friends. Reportedly his drinking and drug use, already at a high level, increased, and he became verbally abusive when provoked even by his closest friends. In his darkest moments George even began to doubt his religion.

Through it all, Olivia proved her loyalty and love, ignoring her lover's boorish behavior and often admonishing him for feeling sorry for himself and to get on with his life. Admittedly it was not easy for Olivia to stand by this difficult, often contrary man and no one would have blamed the young woman if she had bolted. But Olivia was a firm believer, despite their not being legally married, in "for better or worse, in sickness and in health." And so she bit her lip, suffered in silence at her frustration, and she stayed.

Eventually George cautiously ventured back into the recording studio. It was a tentative step. Admittedly, he was still shell-shocked at the failure of *Dark Horse* but, even in the depths of depression, George had been writing and felt that what he had, justified another album. From a purely business point of view, he owed one more album on his Apple contract and with the seemingly never-ending legal entangle-ments with the other members of the Beatles, he was anxious to sever that tie finally, once and for all.

And so it was with widely mixed emotions that he went into the studio to record *Extra Texture (Read All about It)*. The easygoing nature and interplay that had marked previous recording sessions was replaced by a straightforward, largely impersonal approach. The album was technically superior. Emotionally, with such songs as "This Guitar (Can't Keep from Fighting)," "World of Stone," "Tired of Midnight Blue," and "Grey Cloudy Lies," the album was extremely maudlin and fatalistic and largely devoid of the usual reli-gious elements.

Given this reality, it is surprising that *Extra Texture (Read All about It)* did respectably, with the album cracking the Top Twenty in both the U.S. and the U.K. The single "You" did less well, reaching number 20 in America and a disappointing number 38 in the United Kingdom.

Not too surprisingly, there was little call for George to tour, and even less inclination on his part. George took the mediocre showing of *Extra Texture* in stride and returned to a source of solace, tending his garden.

George, now in his mid-thirties, remained very much the reclusive personality into 1976. His public appearances became fewer and farther between. Word began to spread among the few friends George saw, that he was not only emotionally distraught but that physically he was starting to break down. George did not take any of the concerns seri-ously until one morning he absently stared into a mirror. He did not like what he saw.

His eyes were an unhealthy yellow hue. His face was drawn and decidedly thin. He knew in his mind that he had lost a considerable amount of weight. George had to face the fact that he was not well. And in time of crisis, George turned back to religion. George went to guru Paramahansa Yogananda's book *Scientific Healing Affirmations*, a Krishna-based tome postulating that physical ills could be banished through prayer.

Olivia, always the practical member of the partnership, none too delicately insisted that George see a doctor. But George felt that prayer was the answer. And so Olivia watched helplessly as George began chanting a series of mantras designed to restore health. But as the days and weeks went by, and his condition seemed to worsen, George gave in to Olivia's insistence and agreed to be examined by a real doctor.

The news was not good.

The years of physically abusing his body, particularly the ever-increasing use of alcohol and drugs, had resulted in significant liver damage and hepatitis. The doctor prescribed large doses of vitamins. George was scared enough at the diagnosis to immediately give up drinking and drugs. He once again turned to prayer. But his prayers were not answered and his health continued to suffer.

Olivia became frantic at George's physical decline and did extensive research on her own for a possible answer to what had suddenly deteriorated into a life-threatening illness. Finally she contacted a California acupuncturist named Dr. Zion Yu, who had a reputation of being able to cure any malady through this ancient science. George was predictably skeptical when Olivia suggested he see Dr. Yu, but eventually he gave in. The couple traveled to California where George submitted to a series of acupuncture treatments. He noticed an immediate improvement in his physical being and, in a matter of months, was miraculously on the road to a complete recovery.

George's state of mind also began to rebound in 1976. He entered the studio that year to record his next album, and his first for Dark Horse Records, *33⅓*. The tone of the sessions was much more lighthearted and loose than they had been on *Extra Texture*, due in large part to the fact that George had settled into a less pompous and more easygoing approach to songwriting, and the fact that, for the first time in a long time, George was beginning to loosen up and enjoy himself.

Late in December 1975, he had taken the first step in getting back in the public eye when he did a guest spot on the popular BBC television series *Rutland Weekend Television*. In April 1976, he once again traveled to New York City where he sneaked into the chorus of "The Lumberjack Song" during the City Center performance of Monty Python's Flying Circus.

But George's spirits were about to go dark once again.

After years of behind-the-scenes legal wrangling, the lawsuit against George charging plagiarism in the "My Sweet Lord"/"He's So Fine" case had finally reached the courts in January 1976. And so, when he should have been spending his time in the recording studio, George and a literal army of attorneys were spending their days in a crowded, rancorous New York City courtroom, listening with growing agitation and frustration as accusations and half-truths were bantered back and forth.

At one point in the trial, George took the stand and, guitar in hand, explained, in a mind-bending array of technical terms surrounding things like major and minor chords, how the song came into being. In all fairness, George's memory of the origin of "My Sweet Lord" had become vague in the ensuing years. But the story he finally presented to the judge appeared to be a fairy tale, with little reality.

According to legal accounts of the case George, Billy Preston, and a group of faceless musicians and backup singers conceived the early structure of the song while on tour in Copenhagen, Denmark. The transcript further reported that, a week later, George and Preston returned to a London recording studio and, in a recording session that George alleged he did not play on, Billy Preston and some other musicians came up with the basic musical structure of "My Sweet Lord."

Nowhere in this version of the story did George make mention of the backstage jam with Delaney Bramlett, Bonnie Bramlett, and Rita Coolidge. In fact, Delaney's involvement in the scenario was nonexistent. Given that, Delaney was certainly surprised when, at a point during the trial, he received a telephone call from George and his lawyers.

"They wanted me to fly to New York to testify," recalled Delaney. "But I had a previous engagement for the time they wanted me and they couldn't change the time so I couldn't go. So they got in touch with Bonnie and she went and testified. After Bonnie testified, the judge said her testimony was hearsay and didn't allow it."

On September 7, 1976, U.S. District Court Judge Richard Owens found that while he did not feel that George had "deliberately" plagiarized the song "He's So Fine," there was substantial evidence that he did infringe on the song's copyright. George was found guilty and ordered to pay damages in the amount of $587,000.

George was taken aback by the court decision and cynical in his comments in the wake of the decision. "I don't even want to touch the guitar or the piano in case I'm touching somebody's note. Somebody might own that note, so you'd better watch out."

George would put his frustration to good use—composing the song "This Song," a biting bit of satire centered around his legal problems. Unfortunately, the "My Sweet Lord" decision would not be George Harrison's last brush with the legal system.

Dark Horse Records had been only mildly successful to that point, and parent company A&M Records had been counting on George's first Dark Horse release to pull the label into the black. And so when the July 26, 1976, deadline for delivering $33\frac{1}{3}$ came and went, A&M president Jerry Moss was concerned. George assured Moss that the delays were both creative and personal and that he would have the finished master tapes any moment. Two months later George hand-carried the tapes for the album to A&M's Los Angeles offices.

To his shock and surprise, George discovered that A&M was readying a ten-million-dollar lawsuit against him because he had not delivered the album on time. Once he got over the fact that A&M had been quick on the trigger to jeopardize their professional relationship because the album had been late, he made the decision to take his album and his record company elsewhere.

None of this should have come as any surprise to any George Harrison watchers. In his personal and professional life, the temperamental former Beatle had a history of taking offense and burning bridges without too much thought. In the face of the A&M threat, his more ruthless side surfaced. He knew that a former Beatle had a certain amount of cachet, despite a spotty solo career, that any record company would be happy to inherit. And so George took his com-

pleted album across town to Warner Brothers Records and
made them an offer they could not refuse. They could have
the new album and Dark Horse Records if they bought out
his contract obligations with A&M. In return, George agreed
to actively promote the new album with a cross-country promotional tour, something he had been loath to do with previous discs. Warner Bros. agreed and a deal was instantly
struck.

George, on the promotion trail for *33⅓* was a different animal. Alternately witty, insightful, and forthcoming even on
the inevitable and detested questions about the Beatles, he
exhibited none of the long-held beliefs that George Harrison had run from the public never to return. And, it appeared
George was now quite happy being in the spotlight.

A lot of his new attitude rested with the fact that George,
much like his feelings about *All Things Must Pass*, was quite
happy with the collection of love songs and pure pop ditties
on *33⅓*, which eschewed any hint of his religious fervor;
and, as he readily admitted to the press, he was in a much better state of mind than he had been with *Extra Texture*.

Record buyers also saw the change and responded by
making *33⅓* one of George's most popular albums, ultimately spinning off three singles into the upper reaches of
the Top 40.

George was also encouraged later in the year when a
greatest-hits package, *The Best of George Harrison*, was released.
Never what one would consider a Top 40 kind of songwriter, George was rightfully gratified that this selection
pointed out-that he was indeed a songwriter of some talent,
fully capable of creating memorable music.

George was now in a place he had not been in a long time.
Personally and professionally he was in bliss. His physical

health had returned. His love for Olivia had deepened in time. Religion was returning to his life in a much more balanced way and his drinking and drug use was now down to seemingly manageable levels. George was beginning a new phase in his life.

Now was the time to lay his past to rest. He called Eric and Pattie, who in recent years had felt too uncomfortable with the situation to be more than token visitors, and invited himself to their house. After some awkward moments and a few drinks, Eric recalled what happened next.

"George, Pattie, and I were sitting in the hallway of my house. I remember George saying, 'Well, I suppose I'd better divorce her.' He managed to laugh it all off when I thought it was getting pretty hairy. I thought the whole situation was tense, he thought it was funny. That [his attitude] helped us all through the split-up."

George's take on the breakup was consistent with his new mellow attitude. "Well, Eric didn't really run off with her because we had kind of finished with each other anyway. And, you know, for me this is what I think is the main problem. I think the fact that makes the problem is that I didn't get annoyed with him and I think that has always annoyed him. I think that deep down inside he wishes that it really pissed me off but it didn't because I was happy that she went off, because we'd finished together, and it made things easier for me, you see, because otherwise we'd have had to go through all these big rows and divorces."

George and Pattie were officially divorced on June 9, 1977.

George entered a period of quiet reflection. He made occasional odd appearances in various capacities on other people's records, playing an unannounced live set at a local pub, offering congratulations to race-bike driver Barry Sheene on the British TV series *This Is Your Life* and appeared in a cameo role with good buddy Eric Idle (of *Monty Python*) in a send-up of the Beatles—*All You Need Is Cash*—which aired on BBC television.

Easily in one of the most relaxed periods in his life, he was conspicuous by his gracious and outgoing nature in and around his Friar Park home. His first few visits to the local pub, the Row Barge, were a bit uncomfortable as he endured the stares of regulars. But the ice was broken one day when he was invited by one of them to join in a game of darts. He and Olivia became close friends with the bar owner and his wife, Norm and Dot, and would occasionally go out socially with them. Bar habitués were known to be invited to George's house for a home-cooked meal. That he would often pick up the tab for the entire bar was a regular occurrence. He once stopped an interview with a local newspaper reporter to give him an impromptu lesson on guitar.

His personal life became complete in December 1977 when Olivia announced she was pregnant. George was thrilled and, probably, more than a little bit relieved. Although it had become less of an issue with age, George still felt incomplete that he had not had children, and his ego had bridled at the notion that he was the only ex-Beatle that was childless or, even worse, incapable of fathering a child. Now he felt complete.

It was in this rejuvenated state of mind that George stumbled into a second career: film producer.

"It all happened purely by accident," explained George. "An English company had backed out on the Monty Python film *The Life of Brian* in pre-production; and the guys, friends of mine, asked me whether I could think of a way to help them get the film made. I asked my business manager, Denis O'Brien, what he thought and he came back a week later and suggested that we produce it. I let out a laugh. It was a bit risky, I guess, totally stepping out of line for me but, as a big fan of *Monty Python*, my main motive was to see the film get made."

George financed *The Life of Brian*, which went on to be an unexpected commercial success. In short order, Handmade Films was born. George was actively involved in the production of *Time Bandits* and, in the ensuing years, would finance such quirky films as *The Long Good Friday, Mona Lisa*, and *Withnail and I*.

When he was not involved in financing films, George played at being the country squire as he beamed at the sight of Olivia's swelling belly. He spent more time puttering about in his garden and was becoming more sociable, with a steady stream of friends drifting in and out of his home at all hours. George's on-and-off-again romance with race cars once again returned and locals would regularly recall the sight of George spinning around town in his latest acquisition.

Cars were not his only extravagance as he moved into what could best be described as a period of semi-retirement. Although he loved his home in England, he had come to love Australia with its rugged arid lands, and the tropical climes of the island of Maui in Hawaii. So it seemed quite natural to buy houses in both places, which he and Olivia could get away to when the weather turned cold or they needed a change of scenery.

During this period George also began writing songs and preparing to reenter the studio. The songs coming out of George during this time were an unusual amalgamation of thoughts and emotions. The lyrics, as always, were reflective, but this time were full of hope and positive visions. George's religious beliefs were once again uppermost but they were coming out in a simple, rather than heavy-handed manner. Musically, George also seemed inspired as he deviated from the expected elements of rock, pop, and Indian influences and began entertaining highly divergent, often cutting-edge elements. That the album would be titled simply *George Harrison* said a lot about George's feelings about his music and his world. It said that he was confident and happy.

One of the benefits of this quiet time was that George was able to spend a lot of quality time with his father who, at age sixty-five and suffering the effects of a lifetime of smoking, did not have much time left. And so when Harold Harrison finally passed in May 1978, George was predictably saddened but comforted by the time he had been able to spend with him toward the end of his life, and the memories that would linger.

The months of Olivia's pregnancy were a time of great joy and contentment for George. Almost daily he would caress his wife and put his hand on her stomach to feel the kick of life inside her. He kept his business commitments to a bare minimum and was never more than a telephone ring away from Olivia.

With the death of their father, the always good relationship between George and his older brother Harry became even stronger. For a time, Harry had actually moved onto George's estate and was acting as a de facto security guard for the seemingly endless fans who would squeal in delight at the mere sight of George wandering peacefully in his garden.

On August 1, 1978, George, at the advanced age, for fatherhood, of thirty-eight, was a bundle of nervous energy and conflicting emotions as he paced the halls of the Princess

Christian Nursing Home in nearby Windsor. Olivia had gone into labor that day and would give birth to a son. True to the couple's collective spiritual and religious leanings, the child was named Dhani, which is Sanskrit for "wealthy."

George's protective nature immediately escalated upon the birth of his son. George instantly ran out and bought a brand-new Rolls-Royce, colored blue of course, so that his wife and son would not be bounced around on the ride home from the hospital. Overcompensation was the order of the day once the happy family returned to Friar Park. George insisted that his son not leave the house, and even those few friends and relations who were allowed to see the baby were not allowed to touch him. Harry, long used to his younger brother's eccentricity, was astonished by George's latest bit of nuttiness.

"I was a bit surprised," Harry recalled laughingly. "I mean, I've got two kids of my own. But it must have been three or four months before he would even let me touch the baby."

George and Olivia married in a private ceremony on September 2, 1978. It was a simple ceremony, attended only by Olivia's parents. After a joyous honeymoon in Tunisia, George returned to England happy and reenergized, and anxious to get back to the studio.

George's change of musical direction was thoroughly embraced by his fans. The album did respectable if not spectacular business and clearly reinforced George's reputation as the most productive ex-Beatle, and one still quite capable of producing viable music.

Throughout the years, George's relationships with his former mates in the Beatles continued to be varied. The long and winding legal entanglements surrounding the dissolution of the Beatles and Apple Records had soured his relationship with Paul. By the late 1970s, after years of strained phone calls, their feelings toward each other had begun to soften. And once Ringo had gotten over his justifiable anger at George's affair with his wife, the pair amicably made up and became quite close.

George's relationship with John had easily been the most complex and difficult. John's new, often outlandish life with Yoko had long been an irritant to George's more spiritual ways. Musically, they were also often at odds. But through it all they had managed to maintain a strong friendship. They had started out all those years ago as student and teacher. Now that they were equals in all ways, their love for each other was even stronger.

His relationship with Eric and Pattie had also improved. The discomfort they felt in earlier times had not completely gone away, but there was a mutual love and respect that over-rode the darker moments and they were now quite capable of being in each other's company and being comfortable. So much so that when Eric and Pattie decided to get married on March 27, 1979, George and Olivia were at the top of the guest list. For reasons that remain unknown to this day, George and Olivia chose not to attend the wedding.

But when Eric personally extended an invitation to George and Olivia to attend a belated wedding reception on May 19 at Eric's sprawling country estate, they did show up and, according to those present, George was quite gracious in congratulating the happy couple. The party turned out to be an all-star collection of rock-and-roll personalities that included Paul McCartney, Ringo Starr, Mick Jagger, David Bowie, and George's longtime idol, Lonnie Donegan. At one point in the festivities, the assembled musicians mounted a makeshift stage and began an impromptu and, by all reports, a rather sloppy jam session.

It quickly became evident that Eric had succeeded in doing something that nobody else had been able to do; to get three of the four Beatles back together to play. George saw the irony in it all but was having too good a time rocking out to Chuck Berry oldies and the Beatles songs "Sgt. Pepper's Lonely Hearts Club Band," "Magical Mystery Tour," and "Get Back" to think about it all too deeply.

Most saw George's arrival at the party for Eric and Pattie as a not too surprising reflection of George's loving and highly evolved personality and that, in his mind, all things did truly pass. When he heard about that incident, Delaney Bramlett agreed with that assessment but also claimed that, even in the kindest way, George had an ulterior motive.

"That had to be sweet George's slap in the face," he laughed. "In the most positive way, I think it was George's way of getting even. It was his way of saying, 'I've got balls enough to play at your wedding party.' "

eleven

Hide-and-Seek

George had always been a student of what was written about him. It often amused, frustrated, and just plain drove him crazy to watch as the press, as well as the authors of numerous books about the Beatles, as they distorted the facts, played up the sensational, and basically molded his life and times into something with which he was never completely comfortable.

And so, driven largely by ego and the self-assuredness that only he could tell his story, George, in 1979, set out to tell his story his way by writing the autobiography *I, Me Mine*. From the outset, George was not content to do the typical life story. Rather, he chose to pen a quaint, nostalgic look back at his life that was low-key, heartfelt, and, admittedly, insightful and philosophical without the benefit of sleaze, exploitation, and sensation. The book would also contain one-of-a-kind photos from his private collection as well as reproductions of the hand-written lyrics of his favorite songs.

The tone of George's writing was straightforward and whimsical; more a vanity project than anything, so that despite his status as an ex-Beatle the book would not necessarily appeal to the masses. George sensed that and so, rather than approach a mainstream publisher, he chose to publish a limited, signed edition of 2,000 copies (at a cost of a whopping £148 each) when the book was published in August 1979. Eventually the book would find a home with mainstream publisher Simon & Schuster in 1982.

Not unexpectedly, *I, Me, Mine* sold out in record time. Reviews were generally mixed. The one person who took savage exception to George's book was John Lennon.

"I was hurt by George's book," recalled Lennon. "He put a book out privately on his life that, by glaring omission, says that my influence on his life is absolutely zilch and nil. In his book, which is proportedly this clarity of vision of his influence on each song he wrote, he remembers every two-bit sax player or guitarist he met in subsequent years. I'm not in the book. It's a love-hate relationship and I think George still bears resentment toward me for being a daddy who left home. He would not agree with this but that's my feeling about it. I was just hurt. I was just left out as if I didn't exist."

Word of John's displeasure eventually got back to George. In other times, George's answer to John's anger would have been to make an excuse or refuse to answer him at all. But George was in a different place at this point in his life and was legitimately saddened by John's feelings. So much so that, midway through 1980, he called John at his residence at the Dakota Hotel in New York. John was out but George left a message: "Please call George. He's very anxious to talk to you." John's response upon reading the message was, "Well, it's kind of George to call after forgetting to mention me in his book."

John never returned the call.

At about the same time that year, George was once again ready to enter the studio and record the album that would be titled *Somewhere in England*. The executives at Warner Bros.

were particularly happy at the news. While they had taken on the entire Dark Horse label, they knew the reality was that George Harrison would ultimately be the only artist on the roster to turn a profit. They also felt that they had gotten George at his creative and commercial peak and were anxious to strike while the iron was hot.

George was in a mellow, philosophical mood and his religion, in a less fervent but no less positive sense, was once again an influence on his writing and in such songs as "Lay His Head," "Sat Singing," and "Tears of the World." The sessions, featuring a collection of old friends including Ringo Starr, Tom Scott, and Willie Weeks, were an easygoing affair that was finished by the appointed deadline. George was in good spirits when he delivered the master tapes and the surreal cover art. He was sure Warner Bros. would love *Somewhere in England*.

They hated everything about it. They felt the music was uniformly weak, the songs not even remotely commercial. Things were so dire that the WB suits even found the cover art uninteresting. Warner Bros. rejected the album and, in not too delicate terms, told him to go back to the studio and redo it to their satisfaction.

This was the first time that George had faced this kind of creative rejection at the hands of corporate America, and he resented it, so much so that he considered repeating his tactic with A&M that had led him to Warner Bros. But while he would not soon forget the slight and it would color future dealings with the label, George amazingly put his ego aside and willingly went back into the studio, eliminated four songs that had meant a lot to him, replaced them with other songs, and redid the cover art.

On December 9, 1980, George was awakened from a

sound sleep by the telephone ringing. There was a sense of dread as he picked up the receiver. It was his aunt with truly sad news. John Lennon had been shot and killed by an obsessed fan.

George was distraught at the news. He reportedly broke into waves of sobs. His world had been forever destroyed. Shortly after receiving the news, George received another call from the Beatles' former publicist Derek Taylor. Taylor, as delicately as possible, suggested that it would probably be best if George released some statement to the press as soon as possible to avoid being hounded. George was in no mood to be dealing with that chore. He stammered, "I can't now—maybe later," and hung up the phone.

Less than an hour later, the phone rang yet again. It was Derek Taylor, softly insisting that it was in George's best interest that he release some kind of statement as soon as possible. George reluctantly agreed, and the pair hammered out a statement that was dispatched to all the major news agencies that night. It read: "After all we went through together I had and still have great love and respect for John Lennon. I am shocked and stunned. To rob life is the ultimate robbery in life. This perpetual encroachment on other people's space is taken to the limit with the use of a gun. It is an outrage that people can take other people's lives when they obviously haven't got their own lives in order."

The remainder of the night was a surreal series of events. George was suddenly overcome and in a state of terror and panic. His mania for privacy had suddenly burst forth in waves of paranoia. He was concerned that John's death might be the beginning of some dark conspiracy to assassinate all the Beatles. George's grounds manager, responding to George's fears, raced to a shed and emerged with a long length of chain. He moved swiftly to the front of the grounds, slammed shut the wrought iron gates, and wrapped the length of chain around it, securing it from the inside. Word of John's death had spread quickly and a crowd began gathering outside George's home. Despite standing quietly in solemn reverence, there was a sense of unease in the air—which was why George's house manager called the police. Within minutes, a line of squad cars pulled to a stop in front of the property. A number of bobbies emerged and formed a human wall between the rapidly surging crowd and the Harrison mansion.

Inside the house, George stared off into space, chanting quietly.

Later that day, musicians began arriving at George's home, unsure about whether or not George would have the resolve to work. George was totally distracted, awash in the emotions of sadness and fear. But despite suggestions that he might want to take a few days off, George insisted that the best thing for him to do was to go into the studio and continue to work on *Somewhere in England.*

Obviously the sessions from that point onward were extremely somber. Although George would occasionally manage a wan smile when he heard something he liked, for the most part, the reworking of *Somewhere in England,* already a chore in the face of Warner Bros.' rejection, had become a solemn undertaking.

George was casting far and wide in an attempt to pay homage somehow to his slain friend on the album, but his initial attempts at coming up with a fitting musical tribute were coming across as stilted and trite. Finally he turned to a song that was not even on the album's set list, "All Those Years Ago." Originally a song that George had given to Ringo,

George now saw appropriate sentiment and heartfelt emotion in the nostalgic lyrics. He did a quick pass on the song, adding lyrics that reflected his feelings toward John and the tragedy. George felt the tribute would be complete if Paul and Ringo participated in the recording of the song, and so the occasion of the recording of "All Those Years Ago" was bittersweet, with more than a few tears shed. And, in the case of George and Paul, nearly a lifetime of creative and emotional conflicts were at least temporarily put aside as the surviving members of the Beatles gathered to honor a fallen comrade.

Somewhere in England was released in May 1981 and proved to be one of George's most successful albums, rising to number 11 on the U.S. charts and number 13 in the U.K. But George was overjoyed with the fact that "All Those Years Ago," released as a single, rose to number 2 on the American listings and number 13 on the United Kingdom charts.

But by the time *Somewhere in England* hit the charts, George had already dropped from sight. With the death of John and his problems with Warner Bros. still fresh in his mind, the musician pulled back behind the walls of his English mansion, tended to his garden and played at the devoted husband and father. He was the modern equivalent of a feudal lord, entertaining friends such as rock stars Rod Stewart, David Gilmour, and Alvin Lee at home and in pubs and restaurants in and around his neighborhood.

George's on-again, off-again relationship with drugs was back on, with George indulging in hashish, although, according to reports, not to an extreme extent. From a religious perspective, George was also on the move. He was still very much a disciple of Krishna but he seemed to modify his religious journey from the time of John's death. He would chant, but now his banter was more metaphysical than traditional.

Closing in on his fortieth year, George was becoming introspective. The consensus was that he was delving so deep into self that he might not ever return to anything approaching a public life.

Whenever the climate in England turned cold, George would be off to Australia and his home overlooking the Great Barrier Reef or to the two-story mansion that was his Hawaiian retreat. However, the reality was that he could never get far enough away to avoid the paparazzi, who continued to stalk him even in his most private moments, asking inane questions and sticking cameras in his face. In years gone by this would have been an annoyance, but with the death of John Lennon still fresh in his mind, George was constantly in dread of any intrusion on his privacy and would often be rude in the face of even a harmless request for an autograph.

Spending so much of his time in tropical climates was proving to be an inspiration, and soon George found himself writing songs and preparing to return to the studio. It was, however, a creative excitement blunted by the previous problems with Warner Bros., one that made George edgy and defiant as he returned to the recording studio.

George's normally nominal control in the studio slipped into a near-manic case of perfectionism. Songs were being recorded and recorded ad infinitum, and the slightest imperfection, imagined or real, would send George and his group of bemused and frustrated musicians back to the studio to try it again. Long before the sessions that produced the album *Gone Troppo* were completed, the passion had left George, and he was struggling with flagging interest just to get the album completed. By the time George turned in *Gone Troppo,* he did not care. And neither did Warner Bros.

Not that there was anything inherently wrong with the album. The production values were high. The music was well played. In fact, the entire album was nothing if not competent. The problem that Warner Bros. saw was with George's songs. To a one they seemed lyrically lazy and obvious. It was as if the well had gone dry and George had run out of things to say.

The lethargy exhibited by George in not wanting to do anything to promote the album and Warner Bros.' general dissatisfaction with it resulted in *Gone Troppo* literally being dead on arrival. The album went no higher than number 108 on the American charts and the desperation stab at a single, "Wake Up, My Love," stalled at number 53.

George was willing to shoulder some of the blame for the abysmal failure of *Gone Troppo,* citing his unwillingness to jump up and down and be a rock star clown for the sake of selling records. Although possessed of an admittedly healthy ego, the musician was loath at this late date to put it in the direction of what he considered simpleminded publicity. But he was also not letting Warner Bros. off the hook. He claimed that Warner Bros. ignored *Gone Troppo* and did little to promote the record.

No matter who was to blame, George took the failure of *Gone Troppo* as a sign to back away from making music and hinted, in very disillusioned tones, that the leave of absence from the music business might be permanent. "I got a bit tired of it, to tell you the truth. It's one thing making a record but if nobody plays it on the radio, what's the point of spending months in the studio?"

George returned to semi-retirement, putting most of his business acumen to work as a hands-on producer, ramrodding a series of critically successful films for his Handmade production company. Taking a bit of a busman's holiday, George, along with Eric Clapton and Ringo Starr, appeared in a cameo scene from his company's film *Water.* He would also occasionally venture into his home studio and write and record some songs, but those were primarily for his own amusement and not with an eye toward making another record.

Personally, George had seemingly evolved into the perfect domestic. Olivia and he would occasionally go out to dinner with friends or throw a party in their home but, for the most part, were content to stay at home, watch their child grow, and, for George, to get down in the dirt and remove weeds from his garden.

And unlike his marriage to Pattie, George was not imposing his sedentary lifestyle on Olivia. George's wife was a woman of the earth, somebody with simple tastes and simple ideals who saw the home as their own private heaven and was more than willing to live as unglamorous and unencumbered a lifestyle as possible. To say that George and Olivia were on the same wavelength was pure understatement. They were, in fact, true soul mates.

But beneath the seeming tranquillity, there was an angry side to George that was beginning to make its presence felt again. Those in George's inner circle more and more began to see a surly, temperamental man who was likely to lash out in impatience for no reason. George's spiritual and religious identity was again starting to slip and, by 1983, he was almost completely estranged from his friends in the Indian religious and musical community. Olivia was reportedly confused by her husband's recent change of mood but, realizing George was reacting out of boredom and an ongoing sense of not being fulfilled that would be with him forever, encouraged George to stay busy. She had seen her husband like this before, although never with this intensity.

Controversy also began to swirl around the relationship of George and Olivia through the mid-eighties. Although it never amounted to more than rumors stories began to surface that George had reverted to his womanizing ways and that he had had numerous affairs, some rumored to have been under his own roof. George and Olivia would vehemently deny these charges over the years and none could ever be proven.

One very real threat to their marriage was George's return to heavy drug usage and, in particular, cocaine. Reportedly, George had initially attempted to hide his drug use from Olivia but eventually he confronted her with his fondness for cocaine. Olivia took it hard. She was upset that George had been keeping this secret from her and she could not understand why the drug had become such an important part of her husband's life. She hoped George would grow away from the drug and so she stood silently by and hoped for the best.

Many's the night that George would entertain friends with cocaine at his home and would often ring up the neighborhood dealer to bring him more when his stash ran low. Often, at the encouragement of his friends, George was sinking deeper into a drug morass. Although only into his early forties, George was looking much older. His mood swings were notorious and it was apparent that he was slowly but surely slipping into a deep depression.

The reasons for George's descent into hell were many and varied. There was the persistent and haunting specter of John Lennon; his death continued to sit on George's shoulder like a gargoyle. His ego had been damaged by the failure of *Gone Troppo* as well as the fear that he and his music did not matter anymore. But probably the worst calamity for George Harrison in later life was that he no longer had a creative challenge to keep him going from day to day. Was there a cure? Olivia seemed to have the right idea. She loved him but she left him alone, knowing that this was something that George would have to pull out of himself.

How George ultimately pulled out of his funk is open to conjecture. One theory is that George was worried about the impact his depression was having on his wife and son, which, according to those in George's inner circle, was considerable. Another is that George finally rediscovered the joy, rather than the cutthroat dollars and cents side, of music. He began spending more time in his studio and the stream of musician friends stopping by to jam increased.

In recent years, George had been approached on several occasions to play live for a number of benefit concerts, but had respectfully declined. By 1984, however, George was once again anxious to play again. His first opportunity came in December 1984 when, while in Australia for a prolonged stay, he was coaxed by his musician friend Jon Lord to join Lord's band, the heavy metal group Deep Purple, on stage for a couple of numbers. The type of music Deep Purple played was loud and aggressive, definitely not the type of music George preferred. But he was beaming that night as he rocked out like he had not done in years.

In July 1985, the road back continued when, purely on a lark, he recorded the unreleased Bob Dylan song, "I Don't Want to Do It," for the soundtrack for the trashy B sex comedy *Porky's Revenge*. The high point came when he was invited by his lifelong idol, legendary guitarist Carl Perkins, to join an all-star jam on October 21, 1985, celebrating Carl's rockabilly musical life.

"I thought I was wasting my time," recalled Perkins, "because I read he would never go before a live audience anymore."

Perkins was surprised when George readily agreed. George was happy to discover that his old friends Eric Clapton and Ringo Starr had also agreed to perform, which added to his comfort level. Other musicians included Dave Edmunds,

Roseanne Cash, and the members of the then hot rockabilly revival band the Stray Cats. Days before the show George invited all the musicians to his house for a pre-show dinner. That George was totally at ease among his peers was not lost on those musicians who attended the dinner.

"He just opened the door himself, in jeans, a sweater, and his slippers," remembered Roseanne Cash. "He was very sweet. He has a genuine personality that just wants things to be good."

Slim Jim Phantom of the Stray Cats also related how George went out of his way to put everybody at ease. "There's no pretense about him, none."

After a dinner of pasta, mussels, and red wine, the musicians repaired to George's music room where they jammed, playing rockabilly standards until four in the morning.

George's ease turned into a bundle of nerves on the night the Carl Perkins special was taped. Backstage before the show, he was pacing back and forth, tuning and retuning his guitar and, for the first time in a long time, a cigarette was dangling from his lips. When George first hit the stage, he was uptight; barely moving from his spot on the stage and laying down able but unspectacular guitar lines. Perkins was sensing that George had a touch of stage fright, and so he introduced George by yelling out into the audience, "George Harrison, everybody! Don't he look good?" during the song "Everybody's Trying to Be My Baby." George smiled and began to loosen up. For the remainder of the show, it was obvious that George was having fun again.

Slim Jim Phantom raved about George's performance. "He can still play and, man, he sings like a bird. Just fabulous."

Backstage, Olivia watched the show, tears welling up in her eyes. She had not seen her husband this happy in years. Later she would joyously explain, "That's my old George."

twelve

The Big Comeback

George Harrison was indeed the old George again. And in line with his reemergence into the public, he chose to take a big chance with his professional life. He decided to put his money into a film starring Sean Penn and Madonna.

Up to that point, George's Handmade Films had put their money into small, quirky films that seemed destined more for the art house circuit than the mainstream megaplex's. But when Penn and Madonna, after their tempestuous relationship turned into an equally volatile marriage, decided to do a picture together, the romantic comedy adventure called *Shanghai Surprise*, George saw this as an opportunity to cast his production company in a higher profile, and so he willingly invested $15.5 million into the film. On the surface, it seemed like a smart investment, one that would easily turn a profit and put George Harrison, movie producer, back in the public eye.

George was blind to the potential problems. He would soon be courting disaster.

Not long after filming began on *Shanghai Surprise* in Macao, George began getting reports from the set. Sean Penn's bodyguards had beaten a photographer. The film's veteran publicist had been fired by Sean and Madonna for suggesting that the couple take some publicity photos together. George was not used to these kinds of problems on Handmade films, and took it upon himself to travel to Macao to settle things down.

George reportedly got together with Sean and Madonna and gave them a stern lecture on acting like professionals and not causing any unnecessary delays in filming. The two temperamental stars were reportedly so in awe of having a former Beatle reading them the riot act that they backed down from their normal defiant stance and agreed to cooperate. All was fine for a few weeks until the production returned to London, at which point the reports of problems with Sean and Madonna began to filter back to George on a near-daily basis. Reporters and paparazzi were supposedly again being beaten by Sean and Madonna's bodyguards. The petulant couple reportedly refused to work one day when it was discovered that some Polaroids of the fun couple, intended for the film's director, had disappeared. By the time cooler heads prevailed, the production had lost nearly a full day of filming.

Sean and Madonna's attitude toward the press was alarming to George, who had spent his years with the Beatles charming rather than antagonizing the members of the fourth estate. And he was well aware that he would need all the help from the media he could get when *Shanghai Surprise* hit the theaters. So he suggested that the stars of the film meet with assembled press at a conference in London to clear the air of misunderstandings and put the best possible spin on what was already making headlines as a troubled picture.

It was a good idea . . . that went down badly.

Sean Penn decided not to show up, which immediately put the reporters off their feed and George on the defensive. When the press inquired about Sean's absence, George instinctively felt backed against a wall.

"He's busy working," deflected George in a not-too-convincing manner. The interviewers next turned their attention to Madonna, who had showed up, and asked if she and Sean fought. George felt it necessary to step in and answer for Madonna by growling, "Do you row with your wife?" Things began to get totally out of control. The press were focusing in on the personal lives of the film's stars and asking nothing about the film. George could not understand and reproached the press for their negative attitude.

"You're all so busy creating a fuss, then writing about it as if we've created it for publicity," he shot back. When George was challenged, he accused the press of being animals. Needless to say, the press conference dissolved into a combative verbal exchange that would ultimately do more harm than good. When *Shanghai Surprise* opened later that year, the film was roundly panned by critics amid stories of a troubled production and stars out of control.

To say the least, George was disappointed by the experience. It was not the first Handmade film that had received negative reviews, but it had been the first that had been brutally savaged. He had learned that films star's egos were as big and untenable as those of rock stars. And he decided that, for the time being, he did not need that kind of grief in his life. He returned to his role as silent partner–executive producer and vowed never to get too involved in the filmmaking process again.

George returned to his very public seclusion and was once again the subject of much media speculation about his notoriously reclusive lifestyle. George was amused rather than annoyed at the public's overwhelming interest in his private life. "When I tried to keep out of the limelight, people thought it was a gimmick," said George. "They couldn't believe I simply wanted to live like this."

In all fairness, George was slowly emerging into the public life. In March 1986, he joined a high-profile cast of musicians for the charity benefit concert Heartbeat 86, the highlight of which had George sharing vocals with Robert Plant and Denny Laine on a raucous cover of "Johnny B. Goode." Later that same year, George contributed a pair of songs to the comeback album of another one of his childhood idols, Duane Eddy.

George was now inspired and would take any and all opportunities to perform live. While on a short holiday in Los Angeles, he and Bob Dylan went to a local club called The Palomino to see their friend Jesse Ed Davis perform. By the time the dust settled, George and Dylan, along with musicians of note John Fogerty and Taj Mahal, were on stage playing their hearts out in a mammoth, totally spontaneous jam.

A few months later George willingly signed on to perform at the annual charity concert, The Prince's Trust rock concert, at London's Wembley Stadium. When it was announced that Ringo would also participate, the inevitable rumor of a reunion of the surviving Beatles was floated. Paul, as was becoming his wont in recent years, would not do anything involving his former mates. But that did not stop the Prince's Trust show from being a glorious night for George. With Eric Clapton, George played co-lead guitar on a reportedly searing version of "While My Guitar Gently Weeps." George also performed a stirring version of "Here Comes the Sun."

George was again getting the urge to record, but he was leery when it came to choosing a producer. After his bad luck with Phil Spector he was not willing to risk repeating the process and ending up doing all the work himself.

"Who could I possibly work with?" speculated George. "I

don't really know many people who would understand me and my past and have respect for that and who I also have great respect for."

It was suggested by Dave Edmunds that Jeff Lynne, the leader of the very Beatles-inspired Electric Light Orchestra, might be the producer George was looking for. George had heard enough of Lynne's production work on ELO's albums to sense that technically they were on the same wavelength. George suggested that Edmunds contact Lynne and have him call. Lynne contacted George and the pair arranged to have dinner in George's home. The chemistry was good.

"We hung out a bit. The more we got to know each other, it just evolved into this thing. Jeff was the perfect choice. The great thing about Jeff was that he wanted to help me make my record."

Indeed, the sessions for the album that would be called *Cloud Nine* were easily the purest exercise George had ever experienced. Lynne was a constant, prodding, encouraging presence in the studio; encouraging George during songwriting sessions and in assessing instrumental licks for maximum impact. Lynne sensed that George was anxious to leave his spiritual side behind and return to his rock-and-roll roots, and so Lynne steered him in the direction of lean, crisp production with an emphasis on guitar, rhythm, and George's naturally soulful voice.

In Lynne's hands, George was able to fashion an old James Ray blues song, "Got My Mind Set on You," into a modern-day hook-laden pop song primed and ready for radio play. "Devil's Radio" came alive in George's hands as a raging number that indicated that George could still rock with the best of them. There was even a fun-loving, albeit biting satire on George's roots in "When We Was Fab." George could literally not find a a weak song or piece of fluff on the entire disc, and he was elated.

But would Warner Bros. be?

He could not completely put aside the view that Warner Bros. had insulted him on *Gone Troppo*. There was still some underlying anger toward the label and as well as obvious insecurities surrounding the reception *Cloud Nine* would get. In fact, George had been so hinky about dealing with the label that he refused to allow anybody from Warner Bros. to be in the studio or to listen to the finished product. He had promised Warner Bros. that he would deliver the album on August 25, 1987.

On August 25, 1987, a nervous George Harrison, master tape tucked under his arm, walked into the offices of Warner Bros. Lenny Waronker, president of Warner Bros., met George. He was joined a few moments later by Mo Ostin, chairman of the board. This first listen to *Cloud Nine* had suddenly taken on the import of a United Nations summit conference.

After some good-natured small talk, the trio repaired to a listening room. The tension was suddenly thick in the room. The songs on *Cloud Nine* began to fill the room. The looks went from hopeful to joyous. The praise from corporate Warner Bros. was music to George's ears. "Then you mean that I passed the final examination?" said a relieved George. "Well, hooray for that much!"

George was literally on cloud nine as he savored his label's vote of confidence and the promise of massive amounts of promotion, which George eagerly volunteered to boost with numerous interviews and press involvement. George was in such a positive state that when Bob Dylan passed through London on his latest European jaunt, George was not only in attendance but, at Dylan's insistence, he climbed on stage to play with his friend on the Dylan classic "Rainy Day Women #12 & 35."

Cloud Nine was released on November 2, 1987, to near-unanimous raves and massive airplay for the first single, "Got My Mind Set on You." The album went to number 8 in the States while the single rocketed to the top of the charts. George was the recipient of some of his best notices ever, and the stories inevitably touched on the notion that this was George Harrison's big comeback. George read those stories and had a good laugh at the notion that he would need to make a comeback. "People think in terms of a comeback, but I really haven't been anywhere. I've been here the whole time."

George was feeling confident in his own life and career, so much so that he now was more than willing to acknowledge his past life with the Beatles. And so when it was announced that the Beatles would be inducted into the Rock 'n' Roll Hall of Fame on January 20, 1988, George eagerly accepted the opportunity to stand on a dais with Ringo, Julian and Sean Lennon, and Yoko Ono to accept the honors. But the bigger story was that, once again, Paul McCartney refused to show up. Paul released a candid statement stating that, in light of the ongoing legal entanglements between the former band mates, he would have felt like a hypocrite waving and smiling with them.

A more telling truth may well have been that, after years of being the driving creative personality in the Beatles, Paul was now feeling jealous and more than a bit threatened by the resurgent success of George. In fact, while *Cloud Nine* was racking up massive sales and overwhelmingly positive press, Paul's latest effort, *Press to Play*, was failing on a massive scale.

George, in accepting the award, was typically brief in his comments, acknowledging the sadness at John not being with them and making a brief cryptic joke at the expense of Paul's absence. " 'I really don't have much to say," said George that night, "because I'm the quiet Beatle."

George traveled to Los Angeles in April 1988, austensably for a brief vacation and visit with friends and to tie up some business affairs related to the ongoing success of *Cloud Nine*. Of the latter, Warner Bros. was getting ready to release the single "This Is Love" and was looking for a compatible song for the B side. George could not think of any unused material that would be appropriate.

However, during a dinner with Jeff Lynne and their mutual friend legendary rocker Roy Orbison, George explored the idea that it might be fun if the three of them rented some studio time and knocked out an original song together. Lynne suggested that it might be fun if they could record the song in Bob Dylan's studio at his Malibu home. On the day of the session, George swung by Tom Petty's house to borrow a guitar and, reveling in the magic of the session, invited Petty to come along and join in.

It was a magic moment. George and Jeff began writing the music as Petty and Orbison b.s.'d and traded stories and guitar licks. It was not surprising that the four musicians eventually dropped the chore at hand in favor of some good old-fashioned jamming. Dylan, who was watching with bemused curiosity, eventually joined in and an unofficial supergroup was born. Over lunch in Dylan's garden, the five musicians hammered out the lyrics that would ultimately be the song "Handle with Care."

George was so pleased with the finished song, and no doubt reveling in this gathering of rock luminaries, that he felt it would be a waste of a good song to put "Handle with Care" out as a B side. Another song, *"Breath Away from Heaven,"* was quickly substituted. The chemistry had been good. These superstars had been able to check their egos at the door and had been able to create good music. George had a notion. Why not carry this good vibe a step further and record an entire album together?

Thus was born The Traveling Wilburys, a musical hobby that made no pretense to anything but a good time. The ten songs recorded over a little more than three weeks' time were created in a totally relaxed atmosphere in which George acted as the unofficial ringmaster of a group of stellar talents who had turned their collective skills to nothing more than a rock-and-roll good time. As befitting the looseness of the Wilburys, each member took on a fictitious alter ego. George became Nelson, having long ago retired the nom de plume Mysterioso. For the first time since 1969, George Harrison was once again part of a band.

And he was loving every minute of it.

The album, entitled *The Traveling Wilburys: Volume One*, was released in October 1988. Much was made in the pre-release hype of the all-star nature of the group. And while George was all too aware of the amount of press such a pedigreed band would garner, he was more inclined to dismiss the effort as the result of a bunch of blokes getting together for a blow. But once the hype faded, the main factor in the album's success was that the music was an outstanding mixture: pop with an obvious retro bent and guitar-heavy rockers big on harmonies. George's playing and singing was particularly inspired—passionate with a raw, powerful edge.

The album was an immediate commercial hit that ultimately spawned two hit singles, "Handle with Care" and

"End of the Line." There was already talk of a second volume of Wilburys music and, for George, there was the very serious talk of a tour. But for the time being George was content to revel in a job well done and the final coronation of a comeback that could not be denied.

"This is me. I hope I fit in. But I'm not going to lose any sleep over it."

thirteen

Baby, You're a Rich Man

A Traveling Wilburys tour was imminent—until December 6, 1988, when Roy Orbison died suddenly from a massive heart attack. There was talk of going on tour with the surviving members, more as a living tribute to Orbison than a money-making venture. But, ultimately, plans for a tour were put aside, and George went back to living what, by his standards, was a fairly normal life.

"It's different all the time," he once said of his lifestyle. "Like last week I've been just getting up, going for a run around my garden, eat a bowl of oats, and then right into the recording studio. Later go out to dinner, finish off what I was doing, and go to bed. That kind of thing. Varied things, you know. There's no typical day, really."

But with nothing pressing in his professional life, George found ample time to indulge simple musical pleasures. He played on Tom Petty's album *Full Moon Fever* and hooked up with Eric Clapton to add some tasty guitar stylings on the album *Journeyman*. He also contributed the song "Cheer Down" to the soundtrack of the action film *Lethal Weapon 2*. When Olivia became involved in a Romanian aid project for children called Angel, George contributed a Traveling Wilburys' track and a live duet with Paul Simon on the song "Homeward Bound" from a *Saturday Night Live* appearance to the charity album *Nobody's Child*. In 1989, Warner Bros., attempting to squeeze blood from a stone released a collection of Harrison album tracks and unreleased songs entitled *Best of Dark Horse 1976–1989*, which impressed no one and finished at a lowly 132 on the album charts.

In 1990, George reunited with Lynne, Petty, and Dylan for a second round of Traveling Wilburys' play, a light-hearted collection of retro-sounding rockers called *Traveling Wilburys: Volume Three*.

By 1990, George was once again writing, and the consensus was that he would soon be returning to the recording studio, until reality stopped the magic.

Despite having an inquisitive business mind, George was admittedly naïve about the day-to-day running of a multi-million-dollar empire and had, since the end of the Beatles, employed legal and financial advisors to handle investments and other money matters. Denis O'Brien, first as his business manager and later as his co-partner in Handmade Films, had projected a down-to-earth manner as well as a practical business attitude that George trusted implicitly.

But by 1990, the relationship with George and O'Brien was beginning to dissolve amid a growing concern that his business partner, through huge financial investments in a long slate of Handmade Films that all lost money, was not doing things in George's best interest. O'Brien and George eventually parted company in 1993, but the seeds of distrust had already been sowed and so, well before O'Brien left, George was taking over the day-to-day handling of all money matters.

George was suddenly faced with having to handle his own business affairs for the first time in more than twenty years. And it scared him to death. Through fits and starts, George assembled a new team of legal and financial advisors, who set about attempting to make sense of George's messy financial empire. Depending on which scenario one ultimately believes, what they found was startling.

While the figures were murky, in 1991 George Harrison reportedly had an annual income from royalties (from the Beatles and his solo works), shares in what was passing for Apple Records (primarily back catalogue), and personal holdings in the neighborhood of £30–35 million ($70–90 million at the time). This made it all the more astounding when stories began to surface during this period that alleged that George Harrison, through bad business ventures and the gnawing fear that the now-departed O'Brien had misman-aged investments, was close to being destitute.

George would dismiss those reports as rubbish and would jokingly acknowledge that he was not about to be tossed into the street. But, in private, George would admit that there appeared to be a lot less money on the books than there should have been, and that now he was faced with the prob-lem of figuring out just what O'Brien had done and how to go about getting it back.

"Those years from 1991 have been like hell," he angrily confessed in later years. "After all these years of lawyers that I got sucked into after having to handle my own business and finding out what happened to it [the money] after Denis O'Brien abandoned ship, I've hardly picked up a guitar. I'm trying to find the time not to deal with all these accountants and lawyers."

After what George had come to describe as "a real ugly scene," he lapsed into a funk. He was spending more time with accountants than in his home studio. His concentration lapsed. He was returning to his moody ways. Olivia saw what was happening to her husband, but was sadly at a loss about what to do to help him. She reasoned that George needed a positive distraction.

It would come in the form of an invitation from Eric Clapton that he could not refuse. Eric was coming out of a tumultuous period in his own life. His marriage to Pattie did not survive Eric's affair with another woman that produced a son. Tragedy struck early in 1991, when his then four-year-old son Conor slipped out of an open window of an apartment and fell to his death. Eric was looking for something to take his mind off his troubles and, from conversations he had with George, he felt he did, too. Eric's answer was a tour of Japan.

"Everywhere I had toured in recent years, people would always ask about George and when he might tour again. I kept at him, telling him that it would be fun and that there would be no pressure. George had a particularly strong following in Japan and so it seemed perfect."

It was an offer that George seriously considered; especially when Eric offered to head up a band that would serve as his backup band. He had not toured since the disastrous 1974 concerts, and a big part of his psyche was leery of putting himself to the test of a live audience again. But his ego had also been challenged in recent years by the successful tours of Paul and Ringo. What ultimately sold George on touring again was Eric's insistence that he would be backed by a powerful band and that he would be able to rock in a way that he had not done since the heyday of the Beatles.

George and his warm-up act, the Eric Clapton Band, traveled to Japan in December 1991 for the first of a series of twelve concerts. George had drawn up a song list that represented every era of his career as a musician. From his Beatles days, he chose such songs as "I Want to Tell You" and "Tax-man." His solo years were represented by the likes of "Cloud 9," "My Sweet Lord," and "Dark Horse." And from that first show, George was feeling the electricity of being the rocker again.

"It's a good band. It's fun just to be in any band. It's fun after not doing it for so long. It was good of Eric to suggest that we do it."

George's almost childlike enthusiasm during the Japan tour was a voyage of rediscovery that often had his good friend Eric perplexed. "He got a kick out of it at first, but then, when I moved the drummer into a different position, I think he was a bit worried. But I haven't done it very much so I spent a lot of time trying to remember what you do, all the songs to remember and which effect pedal to step on. I did twelve shows and I had twelve chances to get the songs right, so I could improvise some."

The Japan tour proved to be a cathartic experience for George. The reviews were universally good, praising George's relaxed state on stage and the level of excellence of his performance. George suddenly found himself comfortable with his musical past.

"In a way, this sums up my career, it's like a compilation," he explained some months after the conclusion of the Japan tour. "I was very worried about that at first. I hadn't heard these songs since I recorded them because once I record something I never go back to it. Especially the later Beatles songs, we never played them live. So it's a process of reacquaintance. I've found that I like them. A few years ago, I might not have, but now I'm proud of them."

So proud in fact that when it was suggested to George that the tapes of his performances would make a great live album,

George readily agreed and, in his typical perfectionist attitude, found so much that pleased him that when *Live in Japan* was released in July 1992, it was a two-disc set.

Back in England, George continued to struggle with his shaky business empire. O'Brien had been a good friend for a number of years, which made the slow but steady disillusion of their business partnership all the more troubling. But as the details of O'Brien's dealings began to come to light, George's loyalty to O'Brien began to fade. According to legal statements released at the time, O'Brien, while having committed to paying one-half of all the business expenses engendered by Handmade Films, he was, in fact, not paying his half. After extensive searches through literally mounds of financial statements going back years, it was determined that O'Brien's less-than-ethical practices had cost George $25 million.

Throughout 1992 and 1993 George returned to a life of leisure. He would make the occasional appearance on a friend's album and the odd guest on a live show, such as the appearance with Eric Clapton at an April 1992 charity benefit concert. He would also begin to write again, although, at that point, there was too much on his business plate to consider doing another album.

This was also a time of deep meditation and contemplation for George. He was reexamining and reassessing his personal and professional life and had come to be at peace with it all. Especially the Beatles. With age, George had become more philosophical on the subject of the legacy of the Fab Four.

"The history of the Beatles was that we tried to be tasteful with our records and with ourselves. We could have made millions of extra dollars doing all that in the past but we thought it would belittle our image and our songs. I'd like to think we always had a sense of morals about what we did. On behalf of all the remaining ex-Beatles I can say that the fact that we do have some brain cells left and a sense of humor is quite remarkable. I've had my up and downs over the years [with the Beatles] and now I've sort of leveled out."

Midway through the nineties he found himself living a quiet, largely introspective life but one largely devoid of stress. "I spend plenty of time planting trees [around the house]. I have a lot of good friends, good relationships, plenty of laughs. A lot of funny little diversions that keep things interesting."

But while he effectively made peace with his Beatles experience, George, as well as Paul, Ringo, and the Lennon estate presided over by Yoko Ono, were well aware of the impact the group had had on the pop culture landscape. Years after the band's demise, literally hundreds of books, magazine and newspaper articles chronicling various aspects of The Beatles' life and times had appeared. George would grudgingly relate that most of the books had gotten the basic story right, although certain myths and legends had been repeated often enough that they were now passed off as fact, but were frustratingly incomplete because of a lack of cooperation from the surviving Beatles.

Which was why, in late 1993, the Beatles got together and put together an idea for what would be the ultimate and, by their standards, the most factual account of the life and times of the Beatles . . . a mammoth documentary entitled *Anthology.*

"It's really interesting because of the years that elapsed, everybody's put out Beatle footage or videos," said George in explaining the idea behind *Anthology.* "They think they've just about told all the stories, but the real story is the one that only we can tell from our point of view, and we know all the little intimate details. So we've been compiling all this footage from our own cameras and there's just tons and tons of material."

Once the idea for the *Anthology* documentary took place, it was only a small step to agreeing to do an accompanying CD containing outtakes and alternate takes of a number of the Beatles' greatest hits. Almost as an afterthought, the remaining members agreed in principle to write a massive, picture-heavy coffee-table book at some point in the not-too-distant future that would tell the true story of the Beatles.

This was far from an altruistic venture, and it was not too surprising that three of the supposedly richest people on the planet were immediately inundated with offers that would ultimately make them even richer. And it was this element of telling the tale that would give George some uneasy moments.

Because, although it would be nearly a year before his financial difficulties with his former partner would wend their way to a court trial, the speculation about his financial status continued to swirl around him. There had been unsubstantiated reports in the press that George's tour of Japan and the resultant album had been, in fact, a desperation play to generate some quick cash, and now, with rumors of the untold millions that would fill his coffers as the result of *Anthology* and its growing number of offshoots, the same stories were again surfacing with a vengeance. The most vicious was that George was anxious to do *Anthology* in an attempt to keep his home because he was reportedly close to filing bankruptcy. George's response to these outlandish stories was typical George, understated and to the point: "Rubbish."

George had more pressing issues to contend with, such as, could he deal with being around Paul and Ringo that much?

Admittedly, going over old history would be nostalgic and fun, but there were the potential land mines as well such as the not always cordial business dealings between the men and, in particular, the final disillusionment of the Beatles and the ongoing battles over Apple. For George, there would be the revisiting of creative frustrations and the often vicious battles with Paul. *Anthology* would be the sum total of different memories, memories that could reopen old wounds.

As if things could not get more complicated, it was at that point that John Lennon returned from the grave.

John had written and produced primitive demo tapes of the songs "Free as a Bird" and "Real Love" during a creative spurt in the seventies. The simple, erratically produced tapes had, by John's own estimation, been minor bits of work and, consequently, not worthy of inclusion on any of his albums. But Yoko had reexamined the tapes and felt that it would be ironic if the surviving members of the Beatles, along with a big helping of modern studio wizardry, could resurrect these songs as the first legitimate Beatles record since *Let It Be*. George, Paul, and Ringo agreed that it would be a tasteful tribute to John's memory as well as a great marketing ploy for the release of *Anthology*. They also all agreed that Jeff Lynne would be the ideal producer to make this daring experiment work.

Admittedly, all three former Beatles were tentative when they repaired to the studio to re-create Beatles magic with "Free as a Bird" and "Real Love" in 1994. While there in spirit, John's physical absence made for weird, disconnected feelings. There was also the quality of the source material to deal with. The source tapes were ragged first-generation takes; little more than John's often off-key voice and simple guitar backing on a tape conspicuous by its pops and crackles.

Producer Lynne did his best under trying circumstances, tweaking weak tempos and melodies with a nineties technical gloss, patiently dealing with the other musicians' suggestions, and deftly incorporating and cutting in the trio's vocals and, in the case of George, some subtle, cerebral guitar moments. It was therapeutic for George to be back in the studio and it allowed the three former mates to attempt to reestablish some personal rapport. As always, the friction was most evident between Paul and George, which, Paul would later recall, surfaced in the studio and had been typical of their love-hate relationship over the years. "When we were working on "Free as a Bird," there were one or two bits of tension, but it was actually cool for the record. For instance, I had a couple of ideas that he didn't like and he was right. I'm the first one to accept that, so that was okay. We did then say that we might work together but the truth is, after 'Real Love,' I think George had some business problems and it didn't do much for his moods over the last couple of years. He's been having a bit of a hard time actually, he's not been that easy to get on with. I've rung him up and he hasn't rung back. I'll write George a letter and he would not reply to it. It makes me wonder if he actually wants to do it [work together] or not."

Paul's memories aside, the three surviving Beatles went through a period of relative peace during the making of the *Anthology* documentary. There were moments of joy at the memory of the good times, and tight-lipped acknowledgment at what fate had dealt four unknown lads from Liverpool. They were caught up in the enormity of what had been their lives and so, after a particularly grueling day of interviews for the *Anthology* documentary at George's home, they went into George's recording studio and, with only an audience of director Bob Smeaton and a pair of cameramen, performed together for the first time since 1969. Director Smeaton, referring to what has come to be known in Beatles lore as the Friar Park Recordings, said, "There's a whole load of that stuff. They played some old Beatles songs, like 'Thinking of Linking' and that sort of stuff. They did a whole load of rock-and-roll songs and we shot a load of stuff."

However, Beatles spokesman Neil Aspinall tended to downplay the session. "It's really pretty much throwaway stuff. The three of them were just at an interview they were doing at George's place and they just played a couple of things together. It was no big deal. It wasn't like an hour-long jam or anything. They just played a couple of minutes."

No matter the significance of the footage, George has referred to that moment as a fun moment that jogged his memories of the good old days. "It's just some little magic that when you get certain people together it makes fire, or it makes more dynamite. Plus we had good songs, excellent songs, and we were consistent. We were honest, we had a sense of humor and kind of looked quite good at the time. We actually had a sense of being different."

George's renewed feeling for the importance of his Beatle past was rewarded in November 1995 when *Anthology* made its debut on American television. As advertised, the five-hour documentary was a revealing look at the rise and fall of the Beatles and, in the case of George, showed a musician fighting a constant battle against fame and creative frustrations. Not unexpectedly, George had been forthcoming on the ups and downs of Beatlemania and the pressures that ultimately drove the band apart. The premiere of "Free as a Bird" was met with mixed reviews but George was rewarded with much praise for his guitar playing behind John's ghostly vocals.

The praise was the perfect gift as George turned fifty.

George's good cheer was short-lived since, so soon after the airing of *Anthology,* he was once again drawn into a legal battle when his case against Denis O'Brien was finally brought to trial. It was a painful and often embarrassing process as the details of O'Brien's mismanagement of millions of dollars, literally under the nose of George, were revealed in excruciating detail. Finally, in February 1996, a decision was handed down in George's favor and he was awarded an $11.6 million judgment. But it wasn't pretty. In the aftermath of the judge's decision, O'Brien's lawyer accused George of "making all kinds of wild allegations against my client, accusing him of fraud and breach of fiduciary duty that were then dismissed." For his part, the court victory was bittersweet for George who, while receiving the $11.6 million judgment, ultimately had to lay out that much and perhaps more in court costs.

However, George emerged from this latest legal struggle cleansed of any financial concerns or cares, and the press seemed to take their cue from his attitude because, coincidentally, the stories predicting the former Beatles' eminent financial decline stopped.

Seemingly reborn in the nineties as a still vital musician, George took to his newfound prominence with relish, and throughout 1996 was conspicuous by his appearances on other people's records. He was also writing at a furious pace and would predict that another album would be forthcoming in the not-too-distant future. But George's plans were once again sidetracked when he agreed to produce, play, and, yes, sing on his friend Ravi Shankar's latest album, *Chants of India.* *Chants of India* was yet another challenge that George embraced. Rather than simply an album of Shankar playing sitar, this highly experimental outing drew on modern jazz and the more esoteric elements of Indian music for a sound that was both ancient and futuristic.

It had been a while since Ravi and George had worked together, and George was nothing if not excited to be piloting the creative fortunes of his friend. Shankar recalled that "George worked with such love and reverence that I will never forget." Indeed, George was at his most diverse on *Chants of India,* playing the vibraphone, guitar, bass, glockenspiel, autoharp, and marimba. He also contributed background vocals to three of the album's songs. To observers, George had never seemed so expansive in his musical outlook.

What they may have sensed was the fact that George was totally at peace.

fourteen

Black Is Black

George Harrison had a history of not liking doctors, going back to his Beatles days when he would often walk around with a cold or flu and only succumb to a doctor's advice or treatment as a last result. He preferred later years to rely on prayer and the more spiritual elements of Indian mysticism to cure his ills, often with less than successful results.

George knew it was time to consult a physician in July 1997 when, while puttering around in his garden, he discovered a lump on the back of his neck. Fearing it might be cancerous, he checked himself into a hospital and, in a matter of days, the lump was indeed diagnosed as being cancerous and surgically removed. It would be four years later that the notoriously private Beatle would confess to a second bit of surgery in 1997. The removal of part of his lung.

George had been in the very early stages of lung cancer. But the doctors were certain that had gotten to George in time.

"Luckily for me they found that this nodule was more of a warning than anything else," reflected George. "There are many different kinds of cancerous cells and this was a very basic type."

Unfortunately this incident seemed part and parcel of the roller-coaster life of George Harrison. Good periods in his life would inevitably be followed by periods of sickness and/or depression. In many cases they have seemed to coexist. It would not be disclosed until years later that during the period from 1995 to 1996, when George's personal and public life appeared to be on an upswing, his sense of security was being constantly violated.

During the early to mid-nineties, George and Olivia had received numerous death threats in the mail. There had also been several break-in attempts at George's residence that had, fortunately, been stopped. In one of the most extreme cases, FBI reports stated that in 1993 they had intercepted a deranged American arsonist who had made plans to kill George and his family by burning down their house. The irony was that George had made it easy for such attacks to happen.

Since moving into his Friar Park home in the late sixties, George had spent millions of pounds designing his property into an outdoors wonderland. George's insistence of a natural look for his property resulted in the construction of a network of hidden underground passages, caves, and waterways. And while, in the ensuing years, he would spend upward of a million pounds on a high-tech security system, complete with floodlights, video cameras and a cadre of guard dogs and their handlers, the passages and caves were literally left unprotected and offered easy access to any would-be intruder.

The yin and yang of George Harrison's personality was also marked by the fact that, despite his almost paranoid state of mind in regard to security and privacy, he remained the most outgoing of the former Beatles, and the one who would willingly talk to fans. This was pointed up by the fact that George would often be spotted on the streets of Henley on Thames in one of his many cars or walking or having a pint, alone or with a small circle of friends, at the local pub.

Consequently while George seemed hell-bent on guarding his private life he also seemed, perhaps subconsciously so, to be tempting the fates by putting himself in potentially dangerous situations.

But when it came to his health, George seemed, in later years, to acknowledge his vulnerability and to pay attention to any warning signs. And when he did not, Olivia was quick to notice when her husband was looking ill and would point him toward the appropriate treatment.

After his 1997 surgery, George remained in relative seclusion, making the occasional appearance at the local pub but primarily staying at home, playing the house husband and father to the hilt. Visitors to George's home noticed a marked frailty to the musician but assumed it was just the aftermath of his surgery. What they did not know was that, into 1998, George was again feeling ill. So much so that he willingly volunteered to have the doctors take a look at him.

What they discovered was that the cancer had returned, this time settling in his throat.

He was immediately given a massive course of radiation treatment. After the conclusion of the treatment, George's team of physicians announced that the radiation treatment had been successful and that George was on the road to recovery.

"I'm not going to die on you folks just yet," said George in a simple statement to the press following the conclusion of the treatment. "I am very lucky."

Inspired and humbled by his recent bouts with cancer, he plunged full-bore into writing songs. There was a sense of urgency during this period. It was as if George knew his time in the mortal world was coming to a close and that he was at peace with the prospect. His songs were philosophical and autobiographical, spiritual and powerful. During an interview, George felt so comfortable with his new music that he broke his own code of privacy by playing some demos of the new songs "Valentine," "Pisces Fish," and "Brainwashed," which, he told the interviewer, would be on an in-the-works solo album with the title *Portrait of a Leg End*. George was writing as if each and every musical statement might be his last. Going into 1999, George Harrison was truly inspired.

At 3:00 A.M. on the morning of December 30, 1999, George and Olivia were awakened by the sound of breaking glass. Somebody was in the house. George got out of bed and cautiously ventured out into the hallway and down the stairs, where he came face-to-face with thirty-four-year-old Michael Abram, a former heroin addict and mental patient who, according to psychiatric examinations, was convinced that the Beatles were witches and that they were inside his head, telling him what to do. In his hands were a knife and a pole broken off a statue.

George saw the insanity in the intruder's eyes. He did not know what to do. So he began to chant. "I shouted at him, 'Hare Krishna, Hare Krishna.' "

Abram lunged at George with his knife. The seven-inch blade struck George in the chest, barely missing his heart but puncturing a lung. George's chest began to deflate as the blood began to flow from his mouth and the open wound. Summoning up his remaining strength and hoping to keep the attacker from finding his family, George leaped at Abram and the pair engaged in a frantic wrestling match as George's blood spattered the walls.

Hearing the sounds of struggle and her husband's anguished cries for help, Olvia raced out into the hallway, searched for a weapon, and found one in the form of a brass poker. She raced downstairs to discover George bleeding from his wound, attempting to subdue his attacker.

"I've never seen my husband look like that," she would recount in trial testimony. "I raised my hand and hit the man on the back of the head as many times as I could, as hard as I could. My husband said, 'Get him. Get him.' "

Abram turned and knocked Olivia to the ground. But she quickly recovered and continued to beat at Abram's head until he slumped to the ground. By this time, a servant had been awakened by the commotion and had called the police. George and Olivia stood guard over their fallen attacker until the police arrived and took Abram into custody.

George and Olivia were taken to nearby Royal Berkshire Hospital in Reading, where George was admitted at 5:45 A.M. As he watched dazedly as the doctors feverishly worked on him, George was undoubtedly in shock. His decades-old fear of intruders and fatal attacks had finally become a reality.

George was having trouble breathing. The single knife stroke, while fortunately missing any vital organs, had nicked his right lung, causing it to partially collapse. Doctors inserted a drainage tube to remove excess fluid and air from the lung. According to hospital spokesman Mark Gritten, both George and Olivia were "deeply traumatized" by the attack but through it all, George, according to Gritten, had not lost his sense of humor. "At one point he said 'the man wasn't a burglar but that he certainly wasn't auditioning for The Traveling Wilburys.' "

At 3:00 P.M. on the day of the attack, George was transferred to the special chest unit of Harefield Hospital in West London. Olvia, who had received some minor bumps and bruises in the attack, was at George's side. As word of the altercation began to spread, she was being hailed a hero.

"Olivia gave him [Abram] a good clocking," related one of the police on the scene, "and probably saved George's life." A close friend of Olivia's, Elizabeth Emanuel, declared when she heard the news that "she's fit and strong. I imagine she would be very brave in those circumstances. She's quite tough."

George's condition was updated from critical to stable within twenty-four hours of the incident. Harefield Hospital medical director Andrew Pengelly reported that while the knife wound was deep, the blade had missed any major organs. "It could have been a lot worse," he said.

Word of the attack spread around the world in a matter of hours; eliciting responses from many notables in the Beatles universe. Paul McCartney's public statement said, "Thank God that both George and Olivia are all right. I send them all my love. I have no further comment to make." From Ringo came the following: "Both Barbara and I are deeply shocked that this incident has occurred. We send George and Olivia our love and wish George a speedy recovery." Producer George Martin issued this statement. "George leads a very quiet life. He's very down-to-earth. He likes nothing more than doing his garden. George is a very peaceful person who hates violence of any kind." Yoko Ono, speaking for the Lennon estate, stated "My heart goes out to George, Olivia, and Dhani and I hope he will recover quickly."

The press was instantly alive with reports that Paul and Ringo had immediately beefed up their already ample security amid rumors that the attempt on George's life was part of a conspiracy designed to murder the surviving Beatles.

George's condition had improved by December 31. Doctors reported that he was being given antibiotics and pain killers. They also noted that defensive stab wounds and cuts were on George's hands. Further tests and X rays would be performed on January 1 to determine if George was well enough to be discharged. Barring unexpected complications, it was thought George would be fully recovered from his injuries in three weeks. George had, at this point, recovered his sense of humor and was overheard joking with Olivia and the doctors, "I can see the headlines already. George has had a hard day's night."

However, behind the good humor, there were legitimate concerns for George's state of mind. Despite assurances that the wounds on his hands would heal, George was horrified at the prospect of not being able to play music again. Beatle historian Ray Connolly added fuel to the speculation when he was interviewed days after the attack on George.

"He'll be scared, but he's a very cool person," related Connolly. "He has spent a lot of time not being happy having to be a Beatle. Now I think he'll distance himself mentally even further from the idea."

George spent a restful night and was examined once again by doctors on January 1. It was reported that George was progressing and that follow-up X rays had shown a marked improvement. The prognosis for recovery was good but doctors felt it would be best if George stayed in the hospital another week. Late in the evening of January 1, George was secretly discharged from the hospital and went home. At George's request, it was not announced until the next day. And with good reason.

George wanted to avoid any and all publicity inherent to the incident and knew it was going to be difficult. Crowds had already begun gathering at his Friar's Park home and a police presence had been called in to control them. Once home, George lapsed again into a deep depression; feeling vulnerable and fearful at the real horror that had invaded his life. After a few days, George decided that his best bet for peace and quiet was to go to his home in Hawaii.

But George canceled those plans when he discovered that yet another George Harrison stalker, twenty-seven-year-old Cristin Keleher, was arrested December 23 at his Maui home and charged with burglary and theft. When questioned after the arrest, Keleher claimed that she had "a psychic connection" with George.

George retreated into an emotional shell. His one public project during the year 2000 was a simple session gig in which he played a bit of guitar on the song "How Far Have You Come" by the group Rubyhorse. He was once again writing but the consensus was that his recent medical problems coupled with his close brush with death had darkened his mood and outlook. He acknowledged as much during a December 2000 interview in conjunction with the thirtieth anniversary of the release of the album *All Things Must Pass*. "The world is just going mental as far as I'm concerned," said George. "Basically I think the planet is doomed and I think my new songs are an attempt to try and put a bit of a spin on the spiritual side. I'm considering calling my new LP *The Planet Is Doomed Volume 1*."

This was more than mere idle talk on George's part. George had recovered from the attack and was making actual plans to record with an album to be released in November 2001. But the fates were once again about to deal George Harrison another bad hand.

Early in 2001, George began once again to experience fatigue and shortness of breath. By this time, George had become extremely attuned to even the slightest deviation from what he knew to be his normal physical state. He knew he was not feeling right. An examination by a doctor confirmed his worst fears, that a cancerous growth had appeared on one of his lungs.

Under a cloak of extreme secrecy, George flew to the United States in April and entered the Mayo Clinic in Rochester, Minnesota, where he underwent surgery to remove the growth. On May 3, George revealed to the world that he had, in fact, had successful lung cancer surgery and that he was feeling in good spirits and top physical form. "I had a little throat cancer. I had a piece of my lung removed and then I was almost murdered. But I seem to feel stronger. I don't smoke anymore. I'm a little more short of breath then I used to be. So I don't see myself on stage lasting a full fourteen rounds."

George also announced that he and his family would be following his surgery with a vacation in Tuscany. In light of the recent calamities, something about this "vacation" did not ring quite true, and so the media was subsequently alive with all manner of outrageous reports. Some had George being terminally ill and that he had gone off to some secret organization to spend his last days in peace. Others reported that George had actually died and that his burial had been conducted in secret in an attempt to avoid the manic attentions of obsessed fans.

Finally, in June 2001, the truth came out. For the past two months, George had been being treated for a brain tumor at a clinic in the city of Bellinzona in southern Switzerland. During the aggressive series of cobalt-radiotherapy treatments, George had been living in a rented fourteen room hillside home formerly owned by writer Hermann Hesse in Tuscany.

Once word leaked out about his latest illness, George was forthcoming in admitting to the surgery, that it had been successful and that he was "active and feeling very well." But people did not believe him.

The press reports regarding the brain tumor treatment emphasized the seriousness of the malady and, in not-too-subtle terms, hinted at the fact that George was very well near death. This story took on immediate legitimacy when it was reported in the London *Sunday Mail* that George had had a conversation with longtime Beatles producer George Martin in which he had confessed that he fully expected to die soon.

George Martin's manager, Adam Sharp, immediately came forward to angrily deny that the conversation ever took place. George and Olivia released a statement of their own, denouncing the allegations of his impending death as "unsubstantiated, untrue, insensitive, and uncalled for."

However, the denials did not completely quell the speculation on his health or the outpouring of love and emotion directed at George. Thousands of letters were arriving at George's home on a daily basis. Crowds continued to gather in front of his home in silent vigils. On August 5, an informal worldwide moment of prayer was organized in which people were encouraged to stop what they were doing at noon, chant "Hare Krishna" and to play and sing 'My Sweet Lord' as a giant get-well card to George. By all accounts, this demonstration of love toward George was wildly successful.

Although the state of his health would be a constant speculation through the remainder of 2001, those close to George felt he would most definitely survive and prosper. "I am sure he is going to be okay," related George's friend, record producer Bob Rose. "He's a pretty resilient character."

fifteen

Who Am I?

George Harrison had dropped from sight not long after celebrating his fifty-eighth birthday. But there were plenty of fresh footprints to mark his passing.

He surfaced briefly to contribute some minor guitar phrasing to albums by Bill Wyman and the Rhythm Kings, Jim Capaldi, and the reformed Electric Light Orchestra, piloted by his good friend Jeff Lynne.

There were also the rumors that George, still traumatized by the effects of the attack by Michael Abram and absolutely terrified by the news in October 2001 that the relatives of Abram were pushing to have the by-now-institutionalized attacker released and that the legal system was strongly considering it, had put his beloved Friar's Park home up for sale and was spending all of his time out of the country, either at his home in Maui or his villa in Tuscany.

Not that George was in a big hurry. Financially he did not have a care. The success of the various offshoots of the *Anthology* documentary—two more *Anthology* albums and the bestselling book—had swelled his already ample coffers even more. Beyond the money, George, through all the chaos of the past couple of years, had come to find peace in dealing with his legacy as a Beatle. Now he was more forthcoming with stories if people asked. He would occasionally sit by himself and play the old songs and find renewed joy in them.

"The music was always there in the background," he once reminisced, "reflecting our feelings, our desires, and all the things we'd experienced. It goes in leaps and bounds. It's interesting."

George had even managed to stir up some good old-fashioned controversy when, in 2000, while doing interviews for the thirty-year anniversary rerelease of *All Things Must Pass*, he gave a critical lambasting to the current hot band (and Beatle-influenced) Oasis, calling them, among other things, "trite." The band had responded in kind and George, whether he liked it or not, was back in the headlines in a feud that had carried on well into 2001.

There were still the moments of moodiness and it was not too surprising, according to reports, that George was suffering some posttraumatic stress as the result of his near-death experience and his reportedly declining health. George was having his good and bad days. In his mind, nothing was clearly defined.

Which is why, at the end of 2001, just before his death, George Harrison was at the crossroads, professionally and personally, and even he did not seem sure which way to turn.

The on-again, off-again talk of a new album by the end of 2001 never materialized. And while the speculation was that something, however minor, would be forthcoming from George into the new year, the truth was that, as he neared sixty the clamor and the industry buzz of years gone by was dissipating, which may be part and parcel of how historians will view his life in music.

George Harrison had never been a risk taker. A solid if often unspectacular songwriter and a superb, subtle guitar player, George was never one to rock the creative boat or to take inordinate chances with his music. Granted, there have been moments of brilliance over the years. One can always point to *All Things Must Pass* and *Cloud Nine* as moments where his reach happily overextended his tendency to be cautious. But more than one music historian has bemoaned the fact that George Harrison was a classic case of raw talent cutting itself off at the knees, and why is anybody's guess.

The theory of too much too soon seems to hold sway here. George was fulfilled materially and egowise well before the age of thirty. He most certainly never had to work a day in his life by the time the Beatles disbanded, and he seemed, sometimes during what had admittedly been a spotty solo career, to simply be going through the motions. What a hungrier George Harrison might have been able to do will remain a mystery.

Admittedly George had a lot of baggage to carry into his later years. Being a former member of the Beatles was something he could never shake; despite the fact that the truly classic moments from that band belonged to Lennon and McCartney, and perhaps it was a hurdle he could never overcome. Not that fighting the ghost of the Beatles was just George's problem. While a case can be made for McCartney's most commercial moments with Wings, the reality is that only John Lennon produced a consistent body of timeless work in his post-Beatles life; something George had never managed to approach on a consistent basis. And maybe felt he never could.

Because George Harrison was quite simply a creature of

emotions and insecurities. That he wore those elements of his personality on his sleeve were a plus, allowing him to plunge headlong into life's adventures and misadventures without a second thought, in direct contradiction to his creative conservativeness. There was immaturity in George, a cocksureness that was more the foible of youth than of a man who had experienced much in nearly six decades. It led to excess, overindulgence, and a constant dancing in defiance of authority, much as a child might defy a parent. And that, perhaps more than what he accomplished musically, is what people have come to love and admire about him, the quiet but persistent rebelliousness acted out on a world stage.

Which is why it is a good bet that George Harrison did not go Garbo-like into the good night. Yes, he was harder to find in public, his increased paranoia the unfortunate by-product of recent events in his life and the barely suppressed desire to live a quiet, relatively normal life after years in the public eye. He would turn up at the odd session for a friend and the occasional charity bash. There was touring again. No more likely George would be that omniscient presence on the rock music scene, alighting rarely for a live blow with a friend or a one-off unannounced show at a local pub.

George Harrison was most likely a presence turning ever inward in the ensuring years, moving to an even higher spiritual plane, savoring the role of husband and father and reveling in the normalcy of getting his hands dirty in his garden. It is a safe bet that his final years were passed quietly as a lifelong quest for peace, spirituality, and accomplishment.

George seemed to sense this during a 1997 television news interview when, after the inevitable gab about his plans for another album and the anecdote or two about the Beatles, the conversation suddenly took a philosophical turn. It was in that moment that George Harrison, as only he could do, quite succinctly put his entire life in perspective.

"For every human is a quest to find the answer to 'Why are we here? Who am I? Where did I come from? Where am I going?' That, to me, became the only important thing in my life. Everything else is secondary."

The Last Days

George's condition took a turn for the worse in early November 2001. The cancer had returned with a vengeance and was ravaging his already weakened body.

Under a cloak of secrecy, George and Olivia returned to the states and the frail musician checked into New York's Staten Island University Hospital. Friends and family began to gather. In the hands of Dr. Gil Lederman, a pioneer practicing a cancer treatment procedure known as Fractionated Sterotactic Radiosurgery, George was treated with the cutting edge procedure, which uses high doses of radiation to attack cancerous tumors. George's condition was guarded and so speculation ran rampant. More than one rumor broke that George was in fact dead.

On November 8, Elizabeth Freund, a George Harrison spokeswoman, told the press "I'm glad to say he's alive."

But another unnamed source in George's circle stated, "He's hanging on, but it doesn't look good."

George's condition seemingly began to improve in the next 48 hours, to the point where he was discharged from the hospital and was continuing his treatments as an outpatient. The consensus was that while his condition was still guarded, George was improving under the treatment and that his condition was not as grim as when he had first arrived.

George's family began to break their silence on his condition. Pauline Harrison, George's sister-in-law, said that, "We are all very concerned. He is very ill, but putting up a real fight."

Paul McCartney, who was in New York at the time, was extremely saddened by George's declining health and went to the hospital to visit his friend. It was an emotional time for Paul. During the six hour visit, he broke down and wept as he talked with George, now confined to a bed during the treatments. They talked about the past and present, their decades-long feuds and slights dissolving in a veil of tears, good-natured laughter, and wonderful memories. During Paul's visit, George was reportedly in good spirits, knowing in his heart that death was near and bravely preparing to meet his maker. The consensus from those in his inner circle of family and friends was that he was only undergoing the radical treatments to extended his life and the time he had left with Olivia and Dhani.

On November 15, 2001, George, Olivia and Dhani flew out of Newark airport in New Jersey on a private jet headed for Los Angeles and continued treatment at the UCLA Medical Center. While in Los Angeles, George and his family stayed with family friend Gavin de Becker. George's health, despite the continued radiation treatments, continued to decline rapidly during the next ten days and the press was alive with reports on November 25 that George would not live out the week.

According to reports emanating from his inner circle, George was resigned to his fate and was reveling in being in the bosom of his loved ones during his final days. George Harrison was ready to go to God.

George Harrison passed away on November 29, 2001 at 1:30 P.M.

Out of respect to George's devotion to Indian mysticism and Hinduism, George's remains were cremated within hours of his death at the Hollywood Forever Memorial Park. Olivia and Dhani returned to London with George's ashes where formal Hindu rites were performed by two members of the Hari Krishna religious community.

And finally in conjunction with Hindu teachings, Olivia and Dhani traveled to India where, in a pre-dawn ceremony on the banks of the Ganges River, George's ashes were immersed in the water. According to Hindu religion, this final act would allow for the final separation of George Harrison's soul from his body and his spirit to avoid the cycle of reincarnation and to travel straight to heaven.

As his ashes dissolved in the sacred waters of India, the worldwide call went out. George Harrison had gone to his home . . . and was finally at rest.

George Harrison Discography

Albums

WONDERWALL MUSIC (1968)
Microbes; Red Lady Too; Tabla and Pakavaj; In the Park; Drilling a Home; Guru Vandana; Greasy Legs; Ski-ing and Gat Kirwani; Dream Scene; Party Seacombe; Love Scenes; Crying; Cowboy Museum; Fantasy Sequins; Glass Box; On the Bed; Wonderwall; to Be Here; Singing Om.

ELECTRONIC SOUND (1969)
Under the Mersey Wall; No Time or Space.

ALL THINGS MUST PASS (1970)
I'd Have You Anytime; My Sweet Lord; Wah Wah; Isn't It a Pity? (version one); What Is Life?; If Not for You; Behind that Locked Door; Let It Down; Run of the Mill; Beware of Darkness; Apple Scruffs; Ballad of Sir Frankie Crisp (Let It Roll); Awaiting on You All; All Things Must Pass; I Dig Love; Art of Dying; Isn't It a Pity? (version two); Hear Me, Lord; Out of the Blue; It's Johnny's Birthday; Plug Me In; I Remember Jeep; Thanks for the Pepperoni.

THE CONCERT FOR BANGLADESH (1971)
Bangla Dhun; Wah Wah; My Sweet Lord; Awaiting on You All; That's the Way God Planned It; It Don't Come Easy;

Beware of Darkness; While My Guitar Gently Weeps; Jumpin' Jack Flash; Here Comes the Sun; A Hard Rain's Gonna Fall; It Takes a Lot to Laugh/It Takes a Train to Cry; Blownin' in the Wind; Mr. Tambourine Man; Just like a Woman; Something; Bangla Desh.

LIVING IN THE MATERIAL WORLD (1973)

Give Me Love (Give Me Peace on Earth); Sue Me Sue You Blues; The Light that Has Lighted the World; Don't Let Me Wait Too Long; Who Can See It; Living in the Material World; The Lord Loves the One (That Loves the Lord); Be Here Now; Try Some Buy Some; The Day the World Gets Round; That Is All.

DARK HORSE (1974)

Hari's on Tour; Simply Shady; So Sad; Bye Bye Love; Maya Love; Ding Dong; Dark Horse; Far East Man; It Is He (Jai Sri Krishna).

EXTRA TEXTURE (READ ALL ABOUT IT) (1975)

You; The Answer's at the End; This Guitar (Can't Keep from Crying); Ooh Baby (You Know That I Love You); World of Stone; A Bit More of You; Can't Stop Thinking About You; Tired of Midnight Blue; Grey Cloudy Lies; His Name Is Legs (Ladies and Gentlemen).

33⅓ (1976)

Woman Don't You Cry for Me; Dear One; Beautiful Girl; This Song; See Yourself; It's What You Value; True Love; Pure Smokey; Crackerbox Palace; Learning How to Love You.

THE BEST OF GEORGE HARRISON (1976)

Something; If I Needed Someone; Here Comes the Sun; Taxman; Think for Yourself; For You Blue; While My

Guitar Gently Weeps; My Sweet Lord; Give Me Love (Give Me Peace on Earth); You; Bangla Desh; Dark Horse; What Is Life?

GEORGE HARRISON (1979)

Love Comes to Everyone; Not Guilty; Here Comes the Moon; Soft Hearted Hana; Blow Away; Faster; Dark Sweet Lady; Your Love Is Forever; Soft Touch; If You Believe Me.

SOMEWHERE IN ENGLAND (1981)

Blood from a Clone; Unconsciousness Rules; Life Itself; All Those Years Ago; Baltimore Oriole; Teardrops; That Which I Have Lost; Writing's on the Wall; Hong Kong Blues; Save the World.

GONE TROPPO (1982)

Wake Up, My Love; That's the Way It Goes; I Really Love You; Greece; Gone Troppo; Mystical One; Unknown Delight; Baby Don't Run Away; Dream Away; Circles.

CLOUD NINE (1987)

Cloud Nine; That's What It Takes; Fish on the Sand; Just for Today; This Is Love; When We Was Fab; Devil's Radio; Someplace Else, Wreck of the Hesperus; Breath Away from Heaven; Got My Mind Set on You.

TRAVELING WILBURYS: VOLUME ONE (1988)

Handle with Care; Dirty World; Rattled; Last Night; Not Alone Any More; Congratulations; Heading for the Light; Margarita; Tweeter and the Monkey Man; End of the Line.

BEST OF DARK HORSE 1976–1989 (1989)

Poor Little Girl; Blow Away; That's the Way It Goes; Cocka-mamie Business; Wake Up, My Love; Life Itself; Got My Mind Set on You; Crackerbox Palace; Cloud Nine; Here

Comes the Moon; Gone Troppo; When We Was Fab; Love Comes to Everyone; All Those Ages Ago; Cheer Down.

TRAVELING WILBURYS: VOLUME THREE (1990)

She's My Baby; Inside Out; If You Belonged to Me; The Devil's Been Busy; 7 Deadly Sins; Poor House; Where Were You Last Night?; Cool Dry Place; New Blue Moon; You Took My Breath Away; Wilbury Twist.

GEORGE HARRISON LIVE IN JAPAN (1992)

I Want to Tell You; Old Brown Shoe; Taxman; Give Me Love (Give Me Peace on Earth); If I Needed Someone; Something; What Is Life; Dark Horse; Piggies; Got My Mind Set on You; Cloud Nine; Here Comes the Sun; My Sweet Lord; All Those Years Ago; Cheer Down; Devil's Radio; Isn't It a Pity; While My Guitar Gently Weeps; Roll Over Beethoven.

Singles

MY SWEET LORD / ISN'T IT A PITY (1970)

WHAT IS LIFE? / APPLE SCRUFFS (1971)

BANGLA DESH / DEEP BLUE (1971)

GIVE ME LOVE (GIVE ME PEACE ON EARTH) / MISS O'DELL (1973)

DARK HORSE / I DON'T CARE ANYMORE (1974)

DING DONG DING DONG / HARI'S ON TOUR (1974)

YOU / WORLD OF STONE (1975)

THIS GUITAR (CAN'T KEEP FROM CRYING) / MAYA LOVE (1975)

THIS SONG / LEARNING HOW TO LOVE YOU (1976)

CRACKERBOX PALACE / LEARNING HOW TO LOVE YOU (1977)

DARK HORSE / YOU (1977)

BLOW AWAY / SOFT HEARTED HANA (1979)

LOVE COMES TO EVERYONE / SOFT TOUCH (1979)

ALL THOSE YEARS AGO / WRITING'S ON THE WALL (1981)

TEARDROPS / SAVE THE WORLD (1981)

ALL THOSE YEARS AGO / TEARDROPS (1981)

WAKE UP, MY LOVE / GREECE (1982)

I REALLY LOVE YOU / CIRCLES (1983)

I DON'T WANT TO DO IT / QUEEN OF THE HOP (1985)

GOT MY MIND SET ON YOU / LAY HIS HEAD (1987)

WHEN WE WAS FAB / ZIG ZAG (1988)

THIS IS LOVE / BREATH AWAY FROM HEAVEN (1988)

HANDLE WITH CARE / MARGARITA (1988)

END OF THE LINE / CONGRATULATIONS (1989)

GOT MY MIND SET ON YOU / WHEN WE WAS FAB (1989)

CHEER DOWN / THAT'S WHAT IT TAKES (1989)

HANDLE WITH CARE / END OF THE LINE (1990)

WILBURY TWIST / NEW BLUE MOON (1991)

MY SWEET LORD / GIVE ME LOVE (GIVE ME PEACE ON EARTH) (1997)

His Work with Other Artists

LENNON AND MCCARTNEY SONGBOOK

The Silkie (1965)

George played guitar, taps, and tambourine on the song "You've Got to Hide Your Love Away."

CHET ATKINS PICKS ON THE BEATLES

Chet Atkins (1966)

George wrote the liner notes.

YOUNG MASTER OF THE SAROD

Aashish Khan (1967)

George wrote the liner notes.

JAMES TAYLOR

James Taylor (1969)

George sang harmony on the song "Carolina on My Mind"

GOODBYE

Cream (1969)

George co-wrote and played guitar on the song "Badge."

IS THIS WHAT YOU WANT?

Jackie Lomax (1969)

George produced 14 songs on the album and co-produced one. He played guitar and wrote the song "Sour Milk Sea." He played guitar on the songs "Baby You're a Lover," "How Can You Say Goodbye?," "Is This What You Want?," "New Day," "Speak to Me," "Take My Word," "The Eagle Laughs at You," "Won't You Come Back," and "You've Got Me Thinking." George played guitar and contributed backing vocals to the songs "Going Back to Liverpool" and "Thumbin' a Ride."

KING OF FUH / NOBODY KNOWS (SINGLE)

Brute Force (1969)

George remixed the song "King of Fuh."

BLIND FAITH

Blind Faith (1969)

George played guitar on the songs "Exchange and Mart" and "Spending All My Days."

THAT'S THE WAY GOD PLANNED IT

Billy Preston (1969)

George produced the album. He played guitar on the songs "Do What You Want," "She Belongs to Me," "That's the Way God Planned It," "This Is It," and "What about You?" He played sitar on the song "Let Us All Get Together Right Now."

HARE KRISHNA MANTRA / PRAYER TO THE SPIRITUAL MASTERS (SINGLE) (1969)

George played guitar, bass, and harmonium on "Hare Krishna Mantra." He sang backup vocals on "Prayer to the Spiritual Masters."

SONGS FOR A TAILOR

Jack Bruce (1969)

George played guitar on the song "Never Tell Your Mother She's out of Tune."

EVERYTHING'S ALL RIGHT / I WANT TO THANK YOU (SINGLE)

Billy Preston (1969)

George produced the record.

WEDDING ALBUM
John Lennon and Yoko Ono (1969)
George played guitar on the song "Who Has Seen the Wind?"

COLD TURKEY / DON'T WORRY, KYOKO (SINGLE)
John Lennon and Yoko Ono (1969)
George played guitar on both songs.

JOE COCKER!
Joe Cocker (1969)
George played guitar on the song "Something."

ALL THAT I'VE GOT / AS I GET OLDER (SINGLE)
Billy Preston (1969)
George produced the song "All That I've Got." He played guitar on the song "As I Get Older."

INSTANT KARMA / WHO HAS SEEN THE WIND? (SINGLE)
John Lennon and Yoko Ono (1970)
George played guitar and piano on the song "Instant Karma." He played guitar on the song "Who Has Seen the Wind?"

HOW THE WEB WAS WOVEN / FALL INSIDE YOUR EYES (SINGLE)
Jackie Lomax (1970)
George produced both songs.

AIN'T THAT CUTE / VAYA CON DIOS (SINGLE)
Doris Troy (1970)
George produced and co-wrote the song "Ain't That Cute." He co-produced and played guitar on the song "Vaya Con Dios."

GOVINDA / GOVINDA JAI JAI (SINGLE)

The Radha Krishna Temple (1970)

George produced both songs. He played guitar on the song "Govinda."

DELANEY & BONNIE & FRIENDS ON TOUR WITH ERIC CLAPTON

Delaney and Bonnie and Friends (1970)

George, using the pseudonym Mysterioso, played guitar on the songs "Coming Home," "I Don't Want to Discuss It," "A Little Richard Medley," "Only You Know and I Know," "Poor Elijah—Tribute to Johnson," "That's What My Man Is For," "Things Get Better," and "Where There's a Will There's a Way."

JACOB'S LADDER / GET BACK (SINGLE)

Doris Troy (1970)

George co-arranged the song "Jacob's Ladder." He played guitar on the song "Get Back."

MY SWEET LORD / LONG AS I GOT MY BABY

Billy Preston (1970)

George co-produced both songs.

ENCOURAGING WORDS

Billy Preston (1970)

George co-wrote and played guitar and synthesizer on the song "Sing One for the Lord." He played guitar on "All Things Must Pass," "Encouraging Words," "I Don't Want to Pretend," and "My Sweet Lord." He played guitar and sang backing vocals on the song "Right Now." He sang backing vocals on the song "Use What You Got."

DORIS TROY

Doris Troy (1970)

George co-produced the album. He co-arranged the song "Jacob's Ladder." He co-wrote the songs "Ain't That Cute," "Give Me Back My Dynamite," "Gonna Get My Baby Back," and "You Give Me Joy Joy." He played guitar on the songs "Ain't That Cute," "Dearest Darling," "Don't Call Me No More," "Get Back," "Give Me Back My Dynamite," "Gonna Get My Baby Back," "I've Got to Be Strong," "Jacob's Ladder," "So Far," "Vaya Con Dios," and "You Give Me Joy Joy." George also sang backup vocals on the song "Games People Play."

TELL THE TRUTH / ROLL IT OVER (SINGLE)

Derek and the Dominos (1970)

George played guitar and sang backup vocals on the song "Roll It Over." He played guitar on the song "Tell the Truth."

ASHTON, GARDNER AND DYKE

Ashton, Gardner and Dyke (1970)

George co-produced the album. He co-wrote and played guitar on the song "I'm Your Spiritual Breadman."

NEW MORNING

Bob Dylan (1970)

George played guitar on the song "Went to See the Gypsy."

YOKO ONO / PLASTIC ONO BAND

Yoko Ono (1970)

George played sitar on the song "Greenfield Morning I Pushed an Empty Baby Carriage All over the City."

IT DON'T COME EASY (SINGLE)

Ringo Starr (1971)

George produced and wrote the song "It Don't Come Easy."

TRY SOME, BUY SOME / TANDOORI CHICKEN (SINGLE)

Ronnie Spector (1971)

George produced the record. He co-wrote the song "Tandoori Chicken." He played guitar on both songs.

THE RADHA KRSNA TEMPLE

The Radha Krsna Temple (1971)

George produced the album. George and Paul McCartney co-produced the songs "Hare Krsna Mantra" and "Prayer to the Spiritual Masters." George played guitar on the songs "Govinda" and "Sri Isopanisad." He played guitar, bass, and harmonium on the song "Hare Krsna Mantra." He played guitar and tamboura on the song "Sri Guruvastak." He sang backing vocals on the song "Prayer to the Spiritual Masters."

FOOTPRINT

Gary Wright (1971)

George played guitar on the songs "Stand for Our Rights" and "Two-Faced Man."

BOBBY WHITLOCK

Bobby Whitlock (1971)

George played guitar on the songs "A Day Without Jesus," "Back in My Life Again," and "Where There's a Will There's a Way."

JOI BANGLA / OH BHAUGOWAN / RAGA MISHRA JHINJHOTI (SINGLE)

Ravi Shankar (1971)

George produced the record.

IMAGINE

John Lennon (1971)

George played dobro on the song "Crippled Inside." He played guitar on the songs "Gimmie Some Truth," "Oh My Love," "I Don't Wanna Be a Soldier, Mamma, I Don't Wanna Die," and "How Do You Sleep?"

THE BEST

Billy Preston (1971)

George played guitar on the song "I Wrote a Simple Song."

DAY AFTER DAY / MONEY (SINGLE)

Badfinger (1971)

George produced the record.

RAGA (MOVIE SOUNDTRACK)

Various Artists (1971)

George produced the album.

STRAIGHT UP

Badfinger (1971)

George co-produced the album. He played guitar on the songs "Day After Day," "I'd Die, Babe," "Name of the Game," and "Suitcase."

ULULU

Jesse Ed Davis (1972)

George played guitar on his song "Sue Me Sue You Blues"

DAVID BROMBERG

David Bromberg (1972)

George co-wrote and played guitar on the song "The Holdup."

SWEET MUSIC / SONG OF SONGS (SINGLE)

Lon and Derrek Van Eaton (1972)

George produced the song "Sweet Music."

BACK OFF BOOGALOO / BLINDMAN (SINGLE)

Ringo Starr (1972)

George produced and played guitar on the song "Back Off Boogaloo."

SOME TIME IN NEW YORK CITY

John Lennon and Yoko Ono (1972)

George played guitar on the songs "Cold Turkey" and "Don't Worry, Kyoko."

BOBBY KEYS

Bobby Keys (1972)

George played guitar on the song "Bootleg."

SON OF SCHMILSSON

Harry Nilsson (1972)

George played guitar on the song "You're Breakin' My Heart."

BROTHER

Lon and Derrek Van Eaton (1972)

George produced the songs "Sweet Music" and "Another Thought."

TO THE WORLD

Rudy Romero (1972)

George played guitar on the songs "Lovely Lady," "Nothin' Gonna Get You Down," and "Doing the Right Things." He sang on the song "If I Had Time."

DONOVAN RISING

Donovan (1973)

George wrote a verse for the song "Hurdy Gurdy Man" that was not in the original version of the song.

IN CONCERT 1972

Ravi Shankar and Ali Akbar Khan (1973)

George co-produced the record.

THE TIN MAN WAS A DREAMER

Nicky Hopkins (1973)

George played guitar on the songs "Banana Anna," "Edward," "Speed On," and "Waiting for the Band."

CHEECH AND CHONG'S GREATEST HITS

Cheech and Chong (1973)

George played guitar on the song "Basketball Jones Featuring Tyrone Shoelaces."

ERIC CLAPTON'S RAINBOW CONCERT

Eric Clapton (1973)

George co-wrote the song "Badge" and performed it live.

PHOTOGRAPH / DOWN AND OUT (SINGLE)

Ringo Starr (1973)

George co-wrote and played guitar on the song "Photograph." He co-produced the song "Down and Out."

HOBOS, HEROES AND STREET CORNER CLOWNS

Don Nix (1973)

George co-produced the album. He played guitar on the song "I Need You."

IT'S LIKE YOU NEVER LEFT

Dave Mason (1973)

George played guitar on the song "If You've Got Love."

RINGO

Ringo Starr (1973)

George wrote the song "Sunshine Life, for Me" and co-wrote the songs "Photograph" and "You And Me (Babe)." George played guitar on the songs "Photograph," "I'm the Greatest," "Sunshine Life for Me," and "You And Me (Babe)."

ON THE ROAD TO FREEDOM

Alvin Lee and Mylon LeFevre (1973)

George wrote and played guitar on the song "So Sad (No Love of His Own)."

WANTED DEAD OR ALIVE

David Bromberg (1974)

George co-wrote the song "The Holdup."

SON OF DRACULA (SOUNDTRACK)

Harry Nilsson (1974)

George played cowbell on the song "Daybreak."

SHANKAR FAMILY AND FRIENDS

Ravi Shankar (1974)

George produced the album. He played autoharp and guitar on various tracks.

THE PLACE I LOVE

Splinter (1974)

George produced the album. He played guitar on the song "Gravy Train" He played guitar and mandolin on the song "China Light" He played bass and harmonium on the song "Costafine." He played guitar, harmonium, Jew's harp, percussion, and dobro on the song "Drink All Day (Got to Find Your Own Way Home)" He played guitar and percussion on the songs "Haven't Got Time" "Somebody's City," and "The Place I Love." "He played guitar and synthesizer on the song Elly May."

I'VE GOT MY OWN ALBUM TO DO
Ron Wood (1974)
George co-wrote, played guitar and did backing vocals on the song "Far East Man."

IT'S MY PLEASURE
Billy Preston (1975)
George played guitar on the song "That's Life."

HARD TIMES
Peter Skellern (1975)
George played guitar on the song "Make Love Not War."

HARDER TO LIVE
Splinter (1975)
George co-produced the record. He played guitar on the songs "After Five Years" and "Lonely Man."

LUMBERJACK SONG / SPAM SONG (SINGLE)
Monty Python's Flying Circus (1975)
George produced the record.

NEW YORK CONNECTION
Tom Scott (1975)
George played guitar on the song "Appolonia (Foxtrata)."

AIN'T LOVE ENOUGH / THE WHOLE WORLD'S CRAZY (SINGLE)
Attitudes (1975)
George took the picture sleeve photo.

RAVI SHANKAR'S MUSIC FESTIVAL FROM INDIA
Ravi Shankar (1976)
George produced the record.

IN CELEBRATION
  Ravi Shankar (1976)
  George produced the record. He played guitar and auto-harp on and arranged the song "I Am Missing You." He played autoharp on the song "Friar Park."

CROSSWORDS
  Larry Hosford (1976)
  George played guitar on the song "Direct Me." He did backing vocals on the song "Wishing I Could."

ROTOGRAVURE
  Ringo Starr (1976)
  George wrote the song "I'll Still Love You."

ROUND AND ROUND / I'LL BEND FOR YOU (SINGLE)
  Splinter (1977)
  George played guitar on the song "Round and Round."

TWO MAN BAND
  Splinter (1977)
  George was co-executive producer on the record. He played guitar on the song "Round and Round." He played guitar on the song "New York City (Who Am I)."

ALONG THE RED LEDGE
  Daryl Hall and John Oates (1978)
  George played guitar on the song "The Last Time."

MONTY PYTHON'S LIFE OF BRIAN (SOUNDTRACK)
  Monty Python (1979)
  George co-mixed the song "Always Look on the Bright Side of Life."

THE VISITOR

Mick Fleetwood (1981)

George played guitar and sang backing vocals on the song "Walk a Thin Line."

STOP AND SMELL THE ROSES

Ringo Starr (1981)

George wrote, produced, and played guitar and sang vocals on the song "Wrack My Brain." He produced and played guitar on the song "You Belong to Me."

LEAD ME TO THE WATER

Gary Brooker (1982)

George sang backing vocals on the song "The Cycle." He played guitar on the song "Mineral Man."

PORKY'S REVENGE (SOUNDTRACK)

Various Artists (1985)

George sang the Bob Dylan song "I Don't Want to Do It."

WATER (SOUNDTRACK)

Various Artists (1985)

George co-wrote and played guitar on the song "Celebration." He co-wrote the song "Focus of Attention." He played guitar and sang backing vocals on the song "Freedom."

GREENPEACE

Various Artists (1985)

The record includes George's song "Save the World."

DETROIT DIESEL

Alvin Lee (1986)

George played guitar on the song "Talk Don't Bother Me."

BLUE SUEDE SHOES (A ROCKABILLY SESSION WITH
CARL PERKINS AND FRIENDS)

Carl Perkins and Various Artists (1986)

George played guitar and sang vocals on the songs "Blue Moon of Kentucky," "Blue Suede Shoes," "Blue Suede Shoes," "Gone Gone Gone," "Glad All Over," "Gone Gone Gone," "Night Train to Memphis," "Amen," "That's All Right (Mama)," "The World Is Waiting for the Sunrise," "Whole Lotta Shakin' Goin' On," "Your True Love."

MIKE BATT'S THE HUNTING OF THE SNARK

Mike Batt (1986)

George played guitar on the song "Children of the Sky."

TANA MANA

Ravi Shankar (1987)

George played synthesizer and autoharp on various cuts.

DUANE EDDY

Duane Eddy (1987)

George co-produced and played guitar on the songs "The Trembler" and "Theme for Something Really Important."

WITHNAIL AND I (SOUNDTRACK)

Various Artists (1987)

Includes the Beatles song "While My Guitar Gently Weeps," which was written by George.

THE PRINCE'S TRUST CONCERT 1987

Various Artists (1987)

George performed the songs "While My Guitar Gently Weeps" and "Here Comes the Sun."

SONGS BY GEORGE HARRISON (LIMITED-EDITION
BOOK ACCOMPANIED BY AN EP) (1988)

Contains the songs "Lay His Head," "For You Blue," "Flying Hour," and "Sat Singing."

CROSSROADS

Eric Clapton (1988)

George co-wrote and played guitar on the song "Badge,"
He played guitar and sang backing vocals on the song "Roll
It Over." He played guitar on the song "Tell the Truth."

WHO I AM

Gary Wright (1988)

George played guitar on the song "(I Don't Wanna) Hold
Back."

SOME COME RUNNING

Jim Capaldi (1988)

George played guitar on the song "Oh Lord Why Lord?"

GIVE A LITTLE LOVE

Derrek Van Eaton (1988)

George produced the song "Sweet Music."

MYSTERY GIRL

Roy Orbison (1989)

George played guitar on the song "A Love So Beautiful."
He sang backing vocals on the song "You Got It."

FULL MOON FEVER

Tom Petty (1989)

George played guitar and sang backing vocals on the song
"I Won't Back Down."

LETHAL WEAPON 2 (SOUNDTRACK)
Various Artists (1989)
George played and wrote the song "Cheer Down."

RUNAWAY HORSES
Belinda Carlisle (1989)
George played guitar and bass on the song "Deep Deep Ocean." He played guitar on the song "Leave a Light On."

JOURNEYMAN
Eric Clapton (1989)
George wrote and played guitar and sang vocals on "Run So Far."

THE ROYAL CONCERT
Various Artists (1989)
George wrote and performed the songs "While My Guitar Gently Weeps" and "Here Comes the Sun."

WORK IT OUT
Jim Horn (1990)
George played guitar on the song "Take Away the Sadness."

STILL GOT THE BLUES
Gary Moore (1990)
George wrote, co-produced, and played guitar and sang backing vocals on the song "That Kind of Woman."

HELL TO PAY
The Jeff Healey Band (1990)
George played guitar and sang backup vocals on the song "While My Guitar Gently Weeps."

ARMCHAIR THEATRE

Jeff Lynne (1990)

George played guitar and backup vocals on the songs "Every Little Thing" and "Lift Me Up." He played guitar on the songs "September Song" and "Stormy Weather."

NUNS ON THE RUN (SOUNDTRACK)

Various Artists (1990)

Includes George's song "Blow Away."

NOBODY'S CHILD ROMANIAN ANGEL APPEAL

Various Artists (1990)

George wrote and played guitar and sang backup vocals on the song "That Kind of Woman" and the Traveling Wilbury's song "Nobody's Child." George and Paul Simon performed the song "Homeward Bound" from their *Saturday Night Live* performance George played guitar on the Duane Eddy song "The Trembler."

ABOUT LOVE AND LIFE

Vicki Brown (1990)

George played guitar on the song "Lu Le La."

UNDER THE RED SKY

Bob Dylan (1990)

George played guitar on the song "Under the Red Sky."

CALLIN' OUT MY NAME / HOT LOVE WHEN I HAD YOU (SINGLE)

Del Shannon (1991)

George sang backup vocals on the song "Hot Love."

THE BOOTLEG SERIES VOLUMES 1-3, 1961-1991

Bob Dylan (1991)

George played guitar on the song "If Not for You."

HELP YOURSELF
Julian Lennon (1991)
George arranged the guitar on the song "Salt Water."

SONGS BY GEORGE HARRISON 2 (LIMITED-EDITION
BOOK ACCOMPANIED BY EP)
George Harrison
Contains the songs "Tears of the World," "Life Itself,"
"Hottest Gong in Town," and "Hari's on Tour."

GROWING UP IN PUBLIC
Jimmy Nail (1992)
George played guitar on the song "Real Love."

ZOOM
Alvin Lee (1992)
George played guitar on the song "Real Life Blues."

THE BUNBURY TAILS (SOUNDTRACK TO UK CARTOON
SERIES)
Various Artists (1992)
George wrote and performed the song "Ride Rajbun."

THE 30TH ANNIVERSARY CONCERT CELEBRATION
Bob Dylan (1993)
George sang the song "Absolutely Sweet Marie." He
played guitar and sang vocals on the songs "Knockin' on
Heaven's Door," and "My Back Pages."

I HEAR YOU ROCKIN'
Alvin Lee (1994)
George played guitar on the songs "I Want You (She's So
Heavy)" and "The Bluest Blues."

LEON RUSSELL (REMASTERED REISSUE)

Leon Russell (1994)

George played guitar on the songs "Delta Lady" "Prince of Peace," "Indian Girl," "I Put a Spell on You," "Pisces Apple Lady," "Roll Away the Stone," "Shoot Out on the Plantation," and "(The New) Sweet Home Chicago."

FIRST SIGNS OF LIFE

Gary Wright (1995)

George sang backup vocals on the song "Don't Try to Own Me."

IN CELEBRATION: HIGHLIGHTS

Ravi Shankar (1996)

George arranged and played guitar and autoharp on the song "I Am Missing You."

GO CAT GO!

Carl Perkins (1996)

George produced, arranged, mixed and played guitar and bass and sang backup vocals on the song "Distance Makes No Difference in Love."

THE VERY BEST OF ROY ORBISON

Roy Orbison (1997)

George wrote the album liner notes.

CHANTS OF INDIA

Ravi Shankar (1997)

George produced, sang and played various instruments on all tracks.

EVEREST (SOUNDTRACK)

George Harrison (1998)

The score includes a reworking of the George Harrison songs "All Things Must Pass," "Life Itself," "This Is Love,"

"Give Me Love (Give Me Peace on Earth)," and "Here Comes the Sun."

VERTICAL MAN

Ringo Starr (1998)

George played guitar on the songs "King of Broken Hearts" and "I'll Be Fine Everywhere."

HOW FAR HAVE YOU COME

Rubyhorse (2000)

George played guitar on the song "Punchdrunk."

DOUBLE BILL

Bill Wyman and the Rhythm Kings (2001)

George played guitar on the song "Love Letters."

ZOOM

Electric Light Orchestra (2001)

George played guitar on the song "A Long Time Gone."

ANNA JULIA (SINGLE)

Jim Capaldi (2001)

George played guitar on the record.

Bibliography

Interviews

Many thanks to Delaney Bramlett for his time and memories.

Books

Baird, Julia. *John Lennon: My Brother*. Henry Holt, 1988.

Blake, John. *All You Needed Was Love*. Perigee, 1981.

Brown, Peter, and Steven Gaines. *The Love You Make: An Insider's Story of the Beatles*. McGraw Hill, 1983.

Coleman, Ray. *Clapton!* Warner, 1986.

———. *Lennon*. McGraw Hill, 1984.

———. *The Man Who Made the Beatles: An Intimate Biography of Brian Epstein*. McGraw Hill, 1989.

Davies, Hunter. *The Beatles*. W. W. Norton, 1968.

Fast, Julius. *The Beatles: The Real Story*. Berkley, 1968.

Giulliano, Geoffrey. *Dark Horse: The Private Life of George Harrison*. Dutton, 1990.

Goldman, Albert. *The Lives of John Lennon*. William Morrow, 1988.

Harrison, George. *I, Me, Mine*. Simon and Schuster, 1982.

Mala, Raga. *Ravi Shankar: An Autobiography*. Welcome Rain Publishers, 1997.

Martin, George, with William Pearson. *With a Little Help from My Friends: The Making of Sgt. Pepper*. Little Brown, 1994.

Miles, Barry. *Paul McCartney: Many Years from Now*. Henry Holt, 1997.

Norman, Philip. *Shout: The Beatles in Their Generation*. Simon and Schuster, 1981.

Pritchard, David and Alan Lypaght. *The Beatles: An Oral History*. Hyperion, 1998.

Rees, Dafydd and Luke Crampton. *Rock Movers and Shakers*. Billboard Books, 1991.

Schaffner, Nicholas. *The Boys from Liverpool: John, Paul, George, Ringo*. Metheun, 1980.

Seaman, Frederic. *The Last Days of John Lennon*. Birch Lane Press, 1991.

Torres, Ben Fong. *Not Fade Away*. Miller Freeman, 1999.

White, Timothy. *Rock Lives*. Henry Holt, 1990.

Magazines

The Beatles Book, Billboard, Crawdaddy, Current Biography, Film Comment, Goldmine, McCalls, Macleans, Mojo, People, Playboy, Rolling Stone, Undercover.

Newspapers

New York Times, Toronto Sun, New York Daily News.

Television

BBC News, CBS News, VH-1 Interview.

Records

A Conversation with George Harrison (February 15, 2001) Discussing the 30th Anniversary Reissue of All Things Must Pass. Promotional Record.

Web Sites

Beatles Interview Database (www.geocities.com/
  ~beatleboy1/db.menu.html)

  Hari Scruffs (www.hariscruffs.com)

  Jam!Showbiz (www.canoe.ca/Jam/home.html)